FABULOUS FLOWERS

A Coloring Book of
Flowers, Imagination and Symmetry

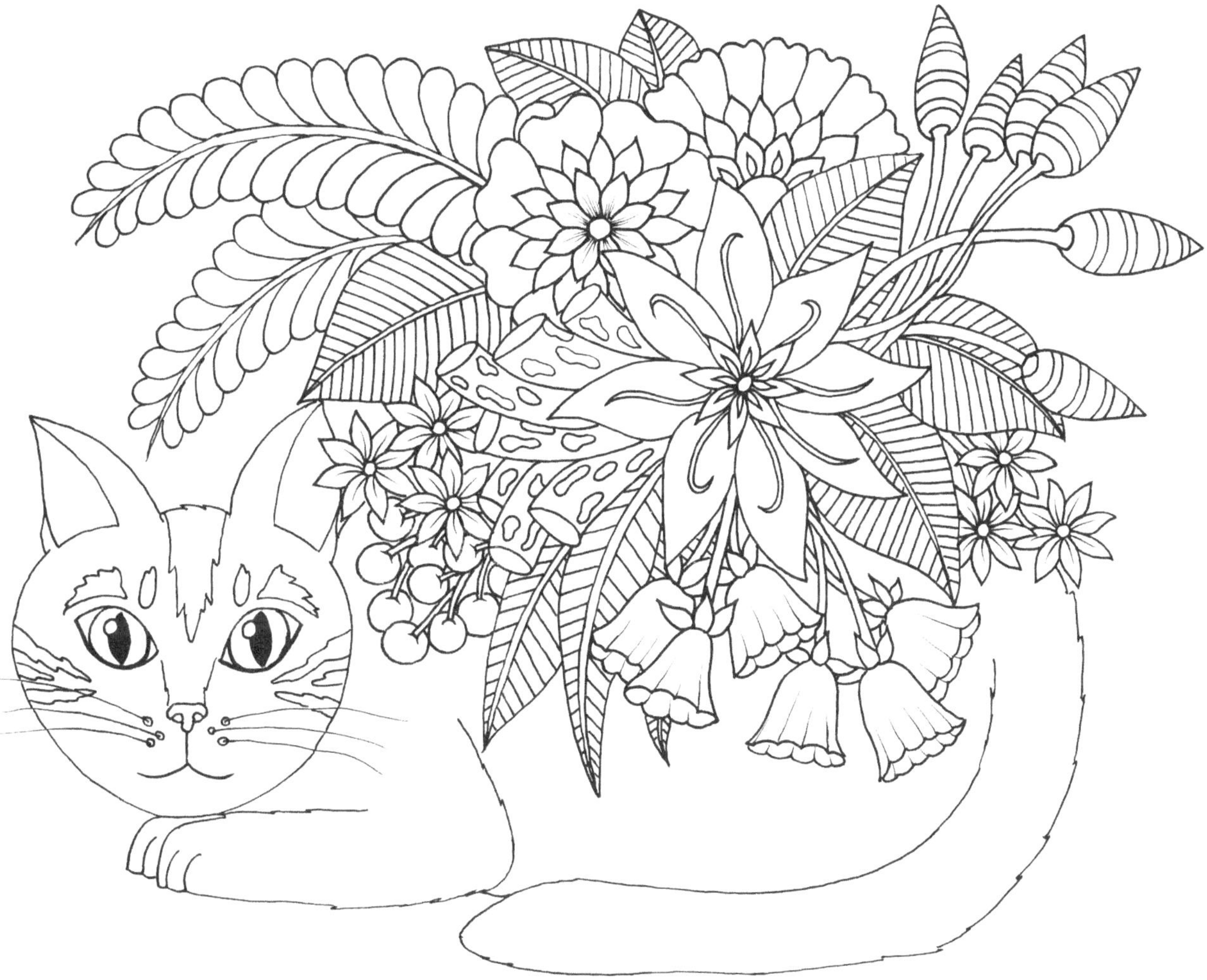

Illustrations by: C. L. Aldridge

Copyright © 2018 C. L. Aldridge

All rights reserved.

In accordance with the U.S. Copyright Act of 1976, the scanning, uploading, and electronic sharing of any part of this book without the permission of the artist/author constitutes unlawful piracy and theft of the artist/author's intellectual property. If you would like to use material from the book (other than for your own personal coloring or review purposes), prior written permission must be obtained by contacting the artist/author at:

CLAldridgeArt@gmail.com

Visit me on Facebook at: www.facebook.com/CLAldridgeArt
Visit my website at: www.CLAldridgeArt.com
Follow me on Twitter and Instagram and YouTube: @CLAldridgeArt

Thank You for your support of the artist/author's rights.

ISBN: 9781730844478

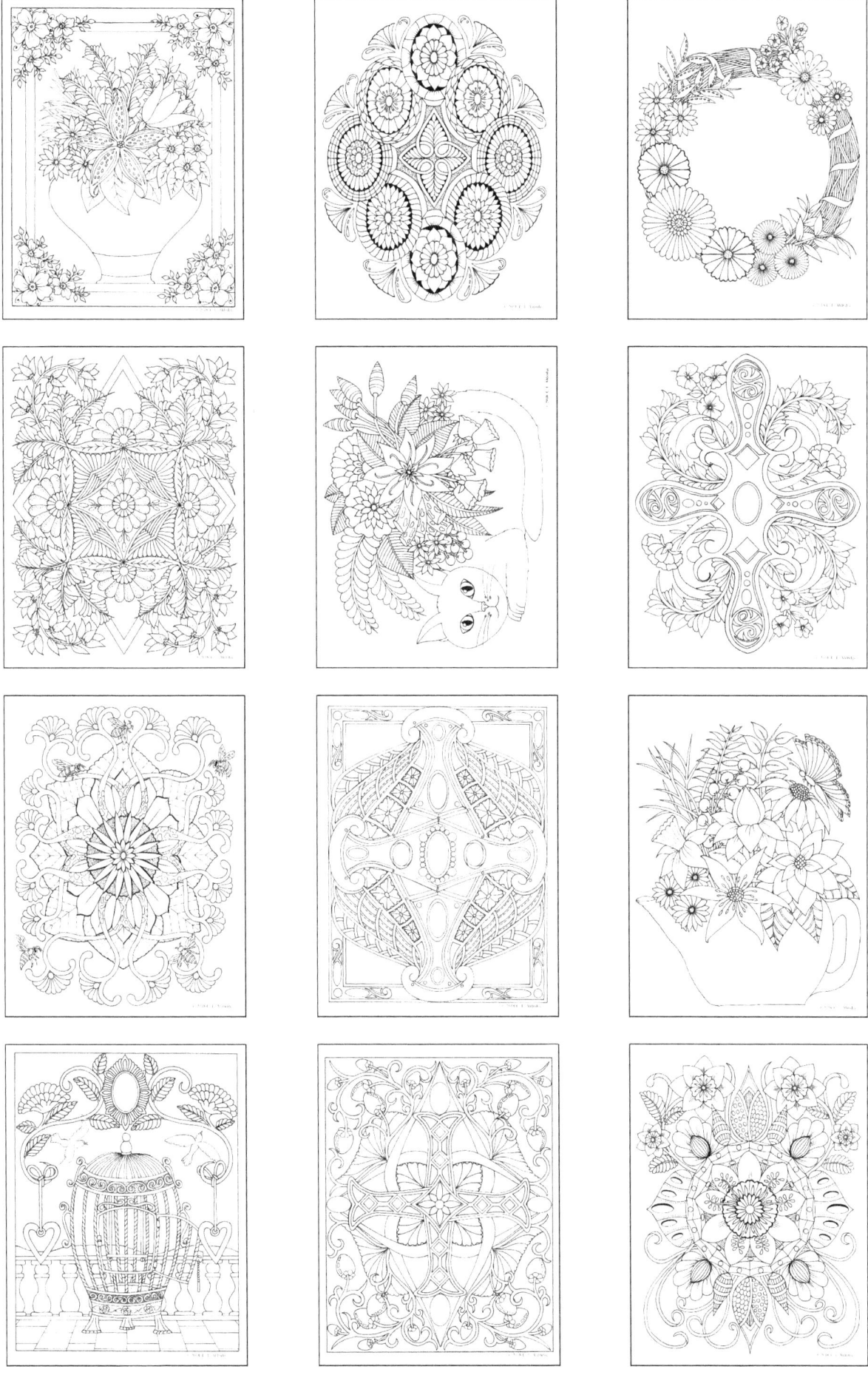

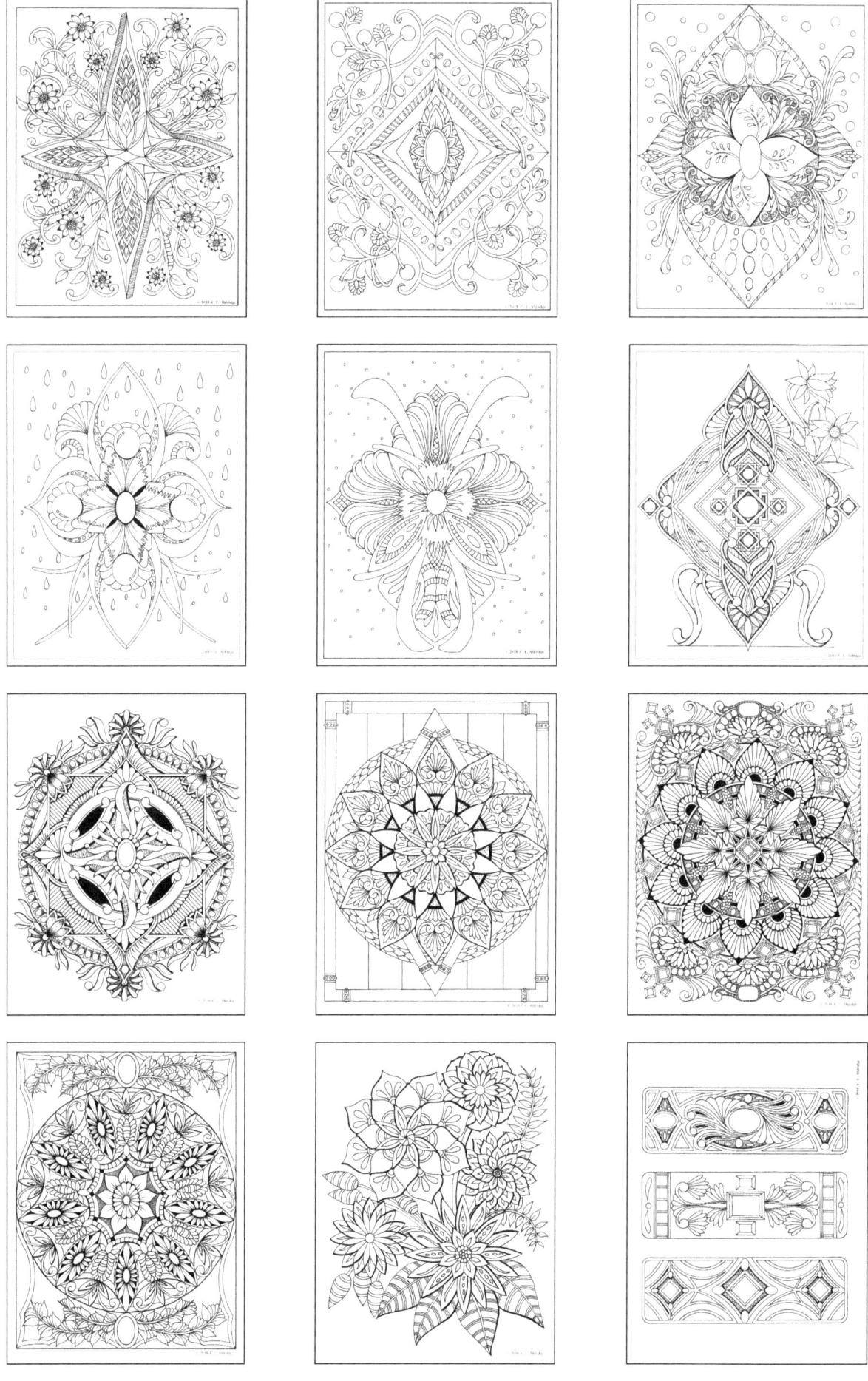

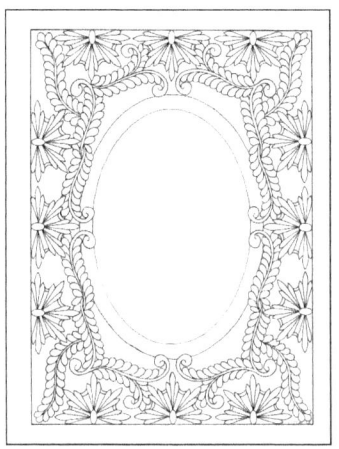
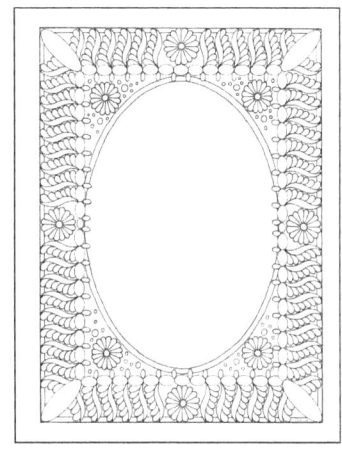

PLUS

A Full set of all 26 drawings in Greeting Card / Crafters size

2 drawings per page

PLUS 5 BONUS PAGES!
A sample from each of the 7 Full Size* Adult Coloring Books by artist C. L. Aldridge.
*Travel Sized 6" x 9" Books excluded

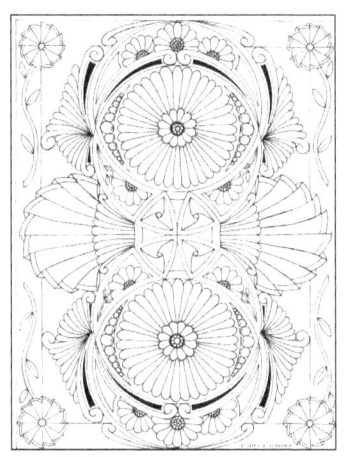

#1 Flowers and Dreams

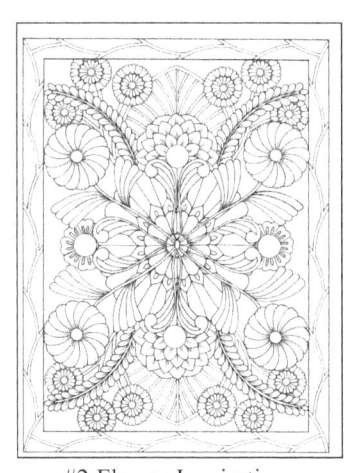

#2 Flower Inspirations

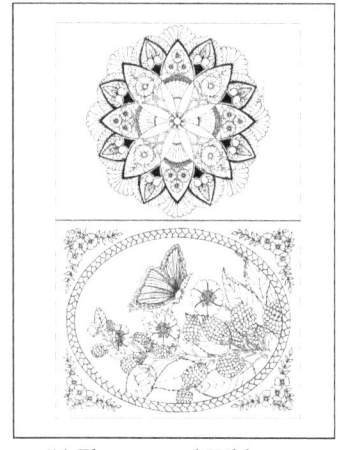

#4 Flowers and Whimsy

#3 Flowers and Flyers

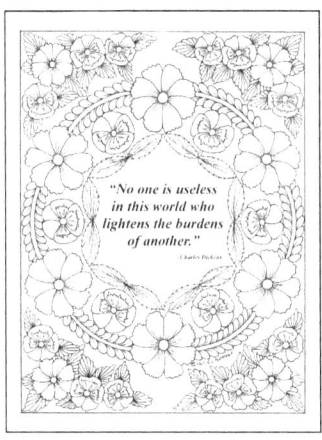

#5 Flowers of Fantasy

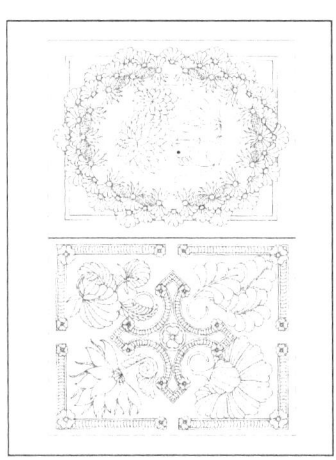

#7 Fantasy Flower Garden

#6 Flowers of Wonder

Also by C. L. Aldridge

Flowers and Dreams
A Coloring Book of Beautiful Botanical Symmetry

Adult Coloring Book of Flower Inspirations
Beautiful Floral Patterns, Botanical Mandalas, Gemstones, Lovely Words and More!

Flowers and Flyers
Adult Coloring Book of Flowers, Songbirds, Hummingbirds, Butterflies, Owls, Ornamentals and More!

Travel Size Book of Flowers, Birds Butterflies and More!
Your Coloring Book for the Road.
(Measures 6" x 9", just the right size to tuck in a purse, a travel bag or a desk drawer.)

Flowers and Whimsy
Adult Coloring Book of Fun to Color Ornamental Floral Patterns, Whimsical Butterflies, Dragonflies and More!

Flowers of Fantasy
A Coloring Book of Fantastical Floral Designs

Flowers of Wonder
A Coloring Book of Fabulous Fantasy Flowers

Fantasy Flower Garden
Adult Coloring book of Fantastic Flowers and Friendly Animals

This book is dedicated to the fans of my work,
who bring such joy to my life everyday; also to Ann Siggers of
A Colorful Life, for introducing me to the extraordinary world
of YouTube videos, as well as her generous and gracious spirit
in reaching out to independent artists. Thank you Mama Fruitbat.

A very special thank you to colorists: Virginia Sanders Cole
and Susan Curry for so generously allowing me to use their colored
renderings of my drawings on the cover of this book.

* * * *

IMPORTANT INFORMATION FOR USING THIS BOOK

- This book contains 26 original design hand-drawn illustrations to color, each is printed SINGLE SIDED (back is blank), PLUS 26 card/crafters size, Plus 7 additional bonus pages (including Title and Belongs To pages, for a total of 61 illustrations to exercise your imagination on!

- Illustrations are printed in TWO SIZES, a full size page and a crafters size (suitable for a 5" x 7" frame, mounting to a greeting card face or scrapbook page, etc). Please note the crafters sizes are also single sided and are printed two on a page.

- The pages are printed on #60 lb bright white paper which performs well for all brands of colored pencils and crayons, without the need of a blotter page.

- To avoid any "Uh Oh's" and the associated disappointment, **Marker and Gel Pen users are STRONGLY ENCOURAGED to USE A BLOTTER SHEET** behind the drawing to avoid any possibility of bleed through to the next page. Several blank blotter and color testing pages are provided at the end of this book.

- Most IMPORTANT of all: Relax, have fun, stand-up and stretch often, and remember that sometimes the most beautiful things come from what we think at first are mistakes, but which turn out to be art's way of working magic!

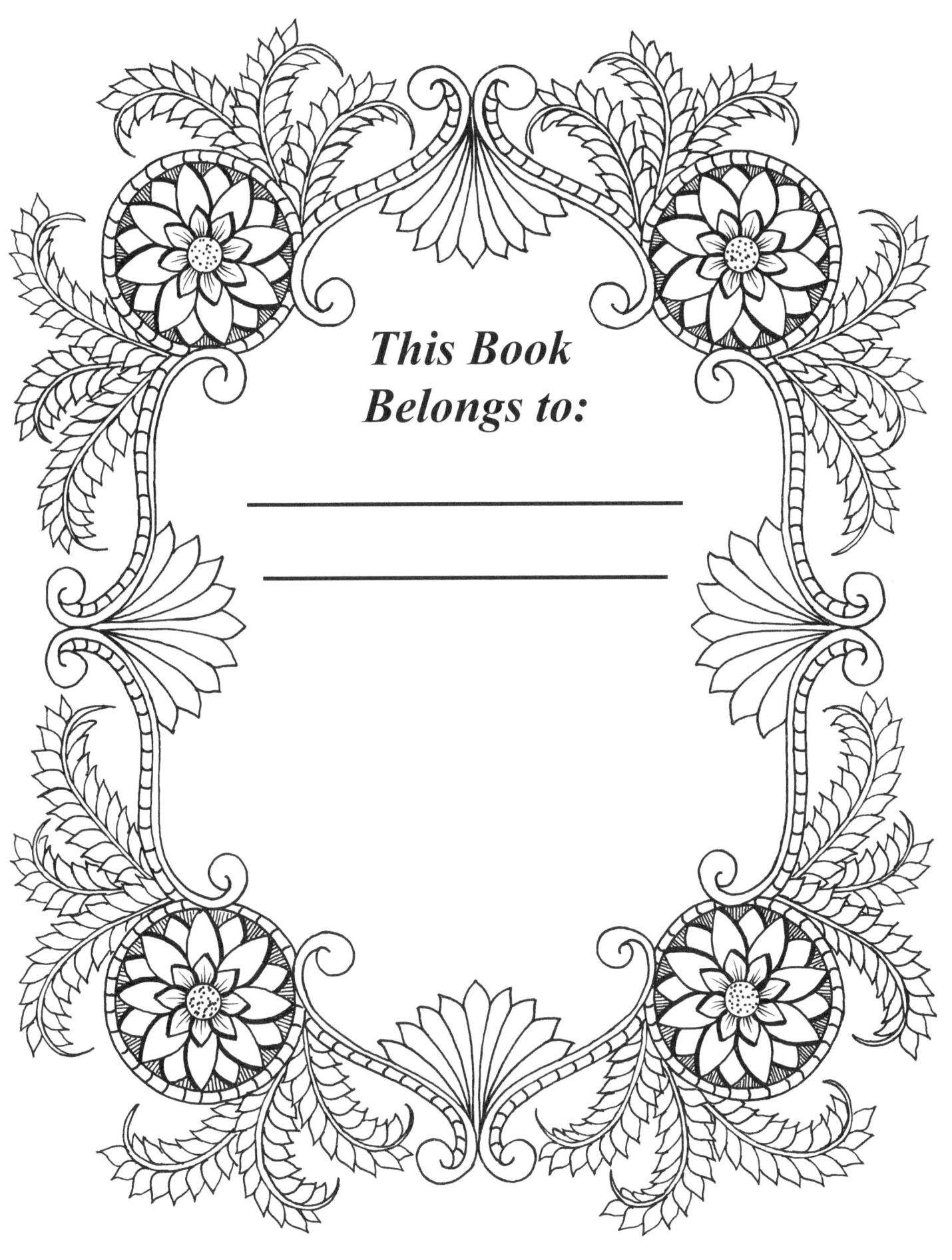

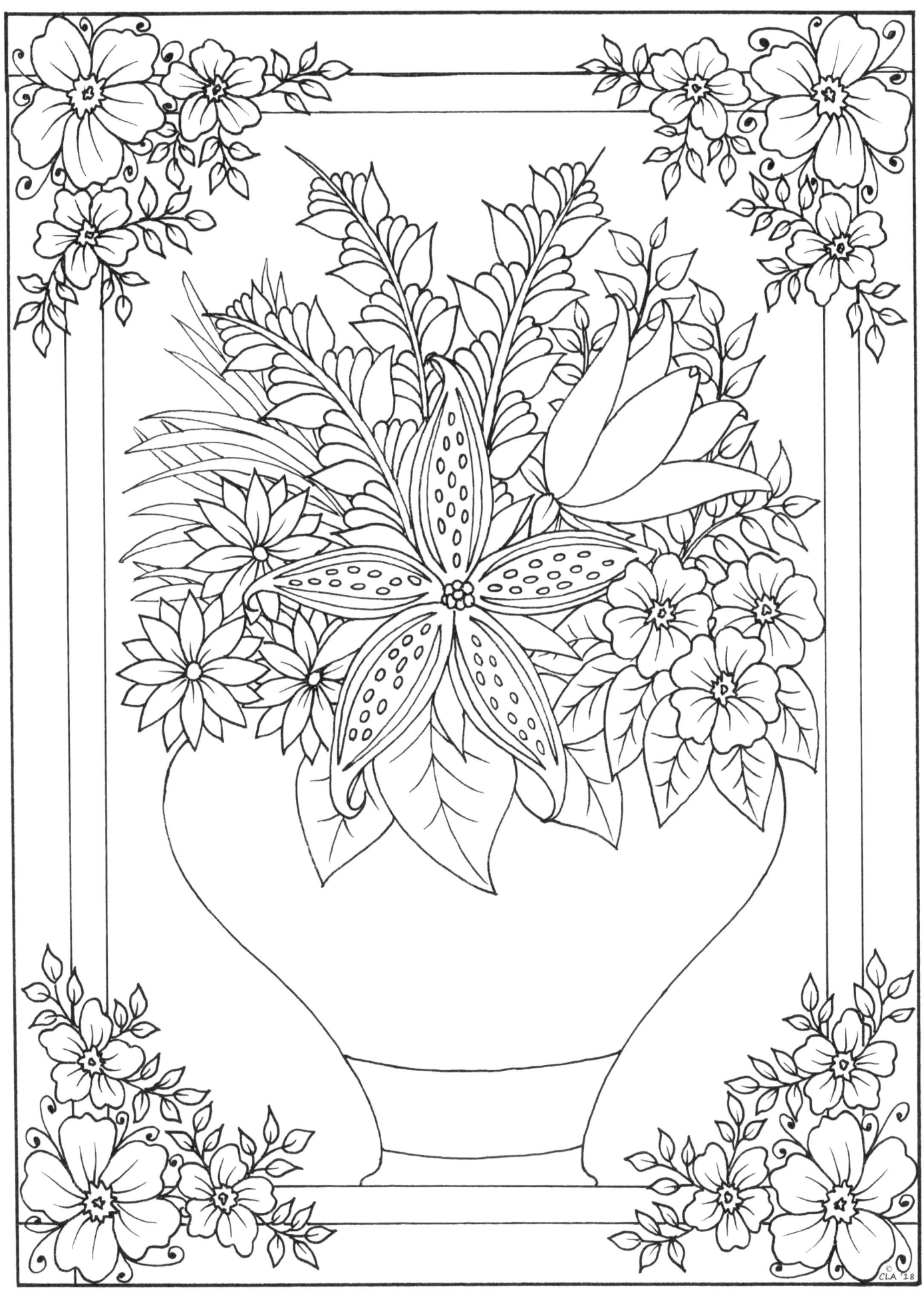

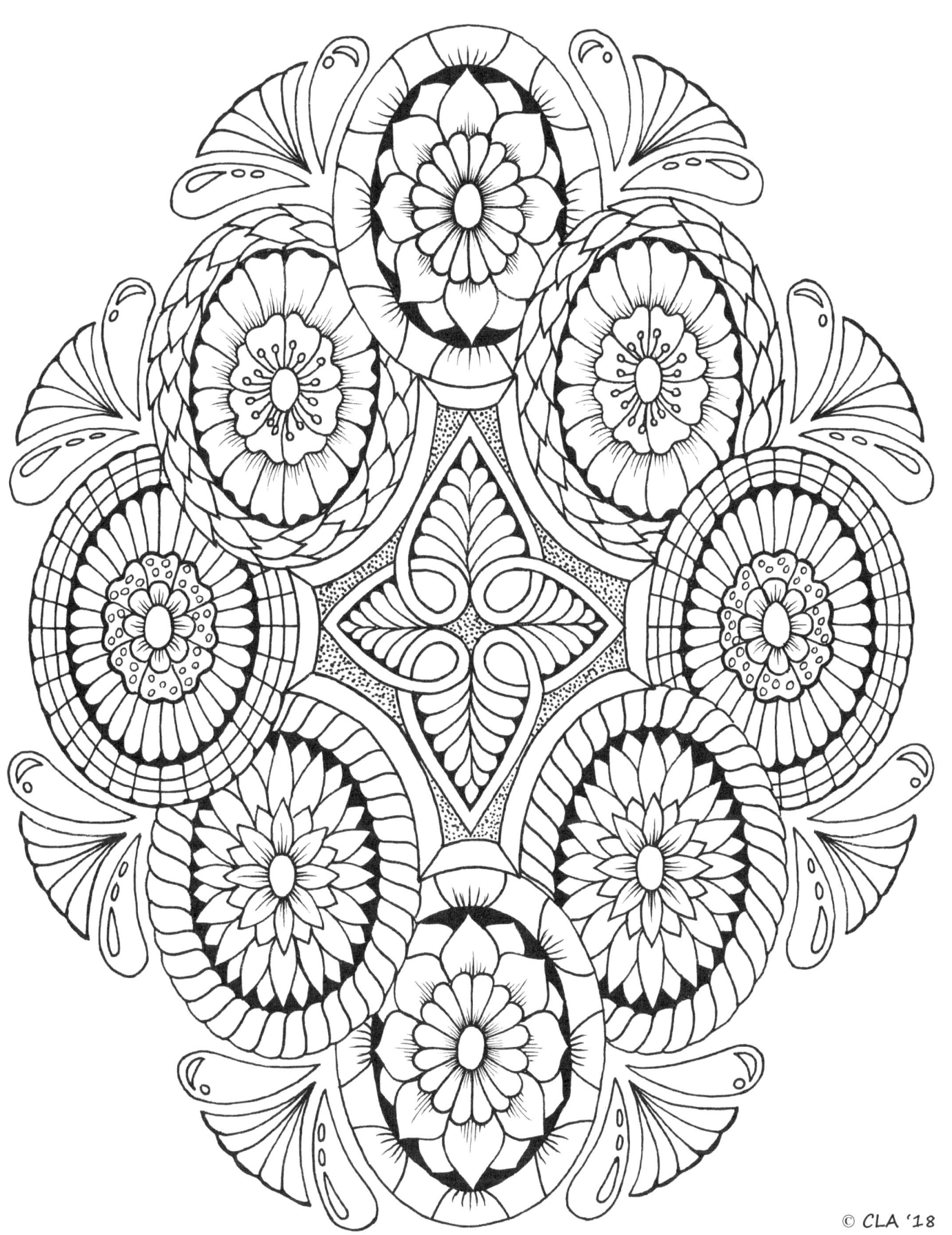

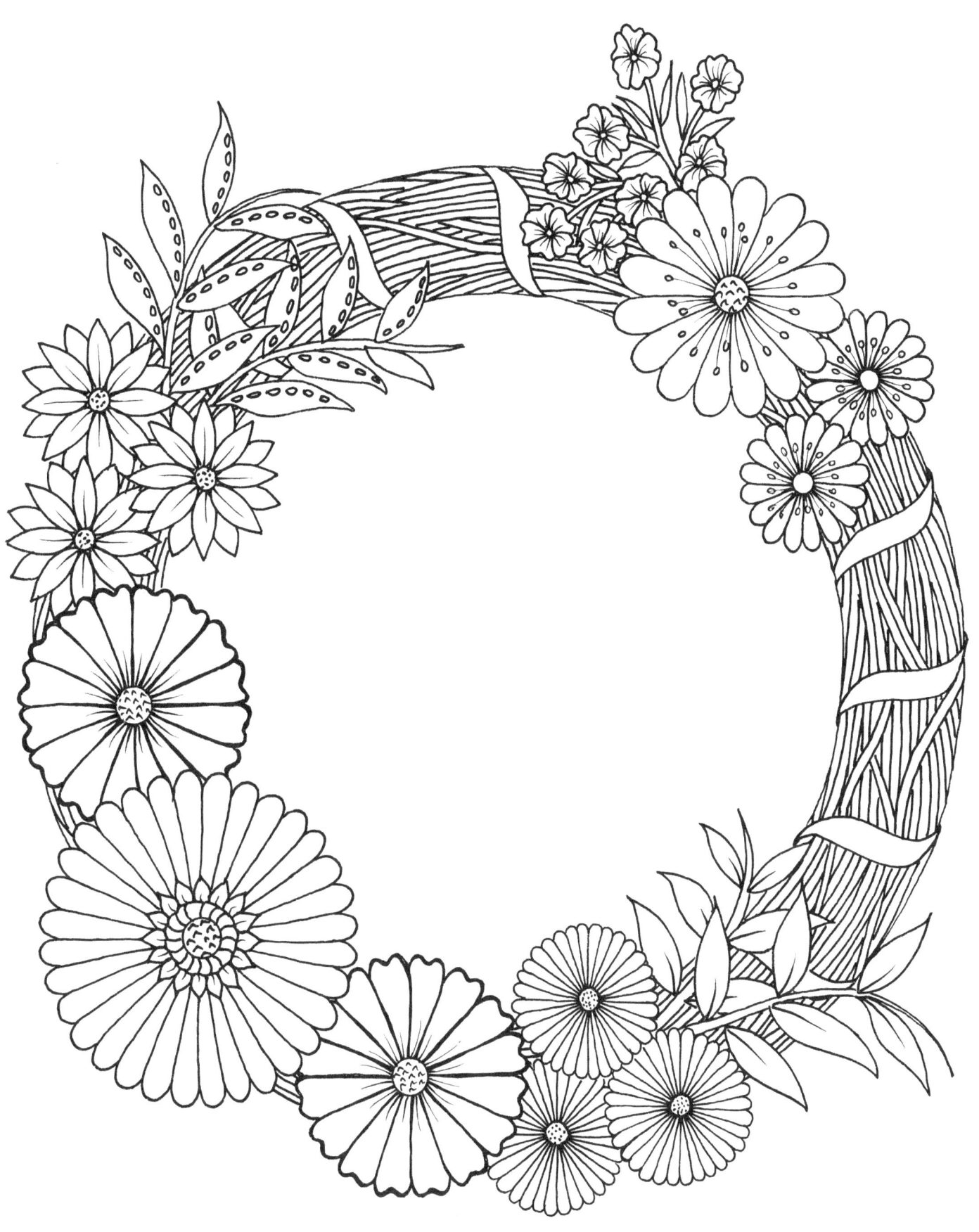

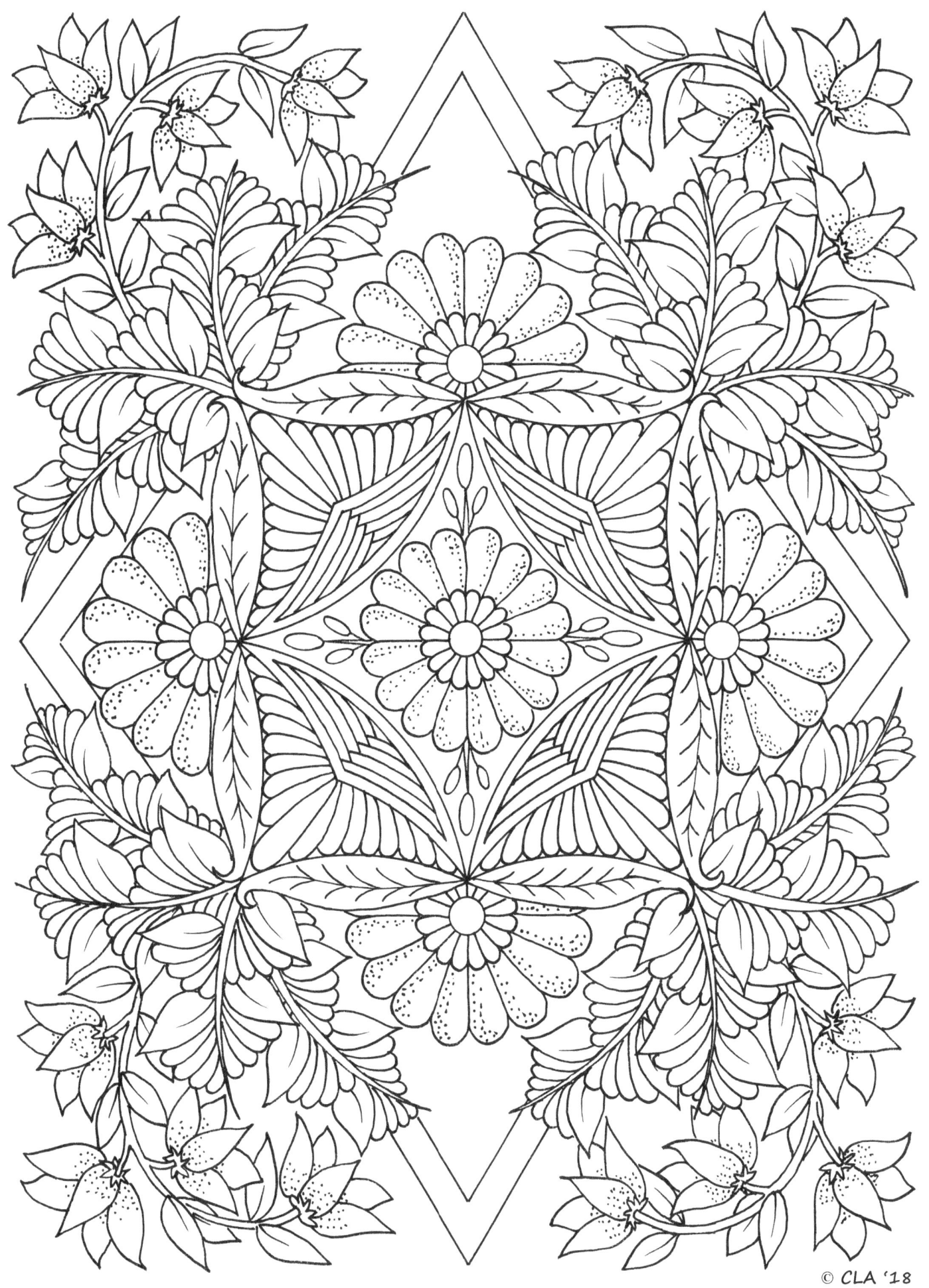

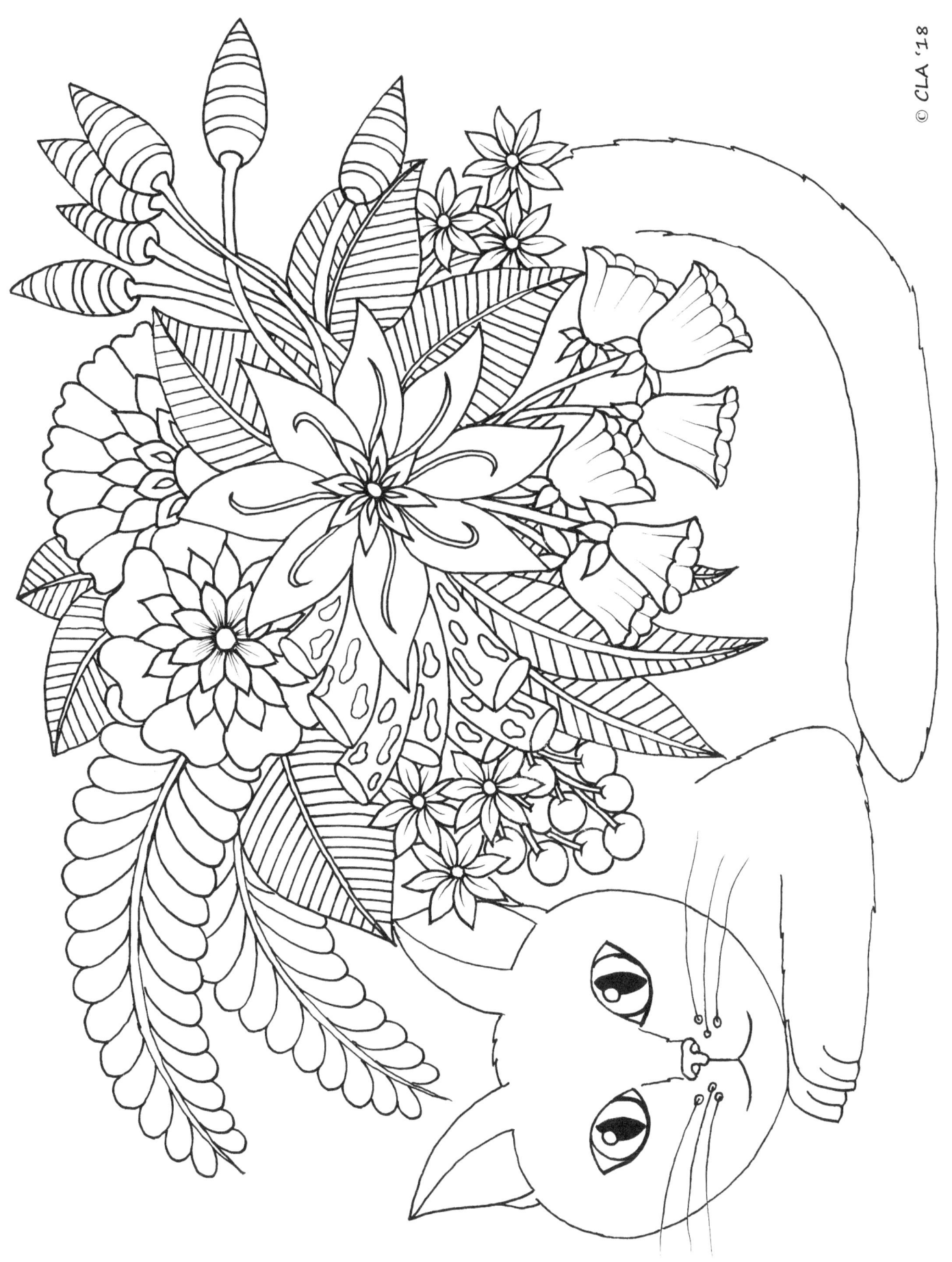

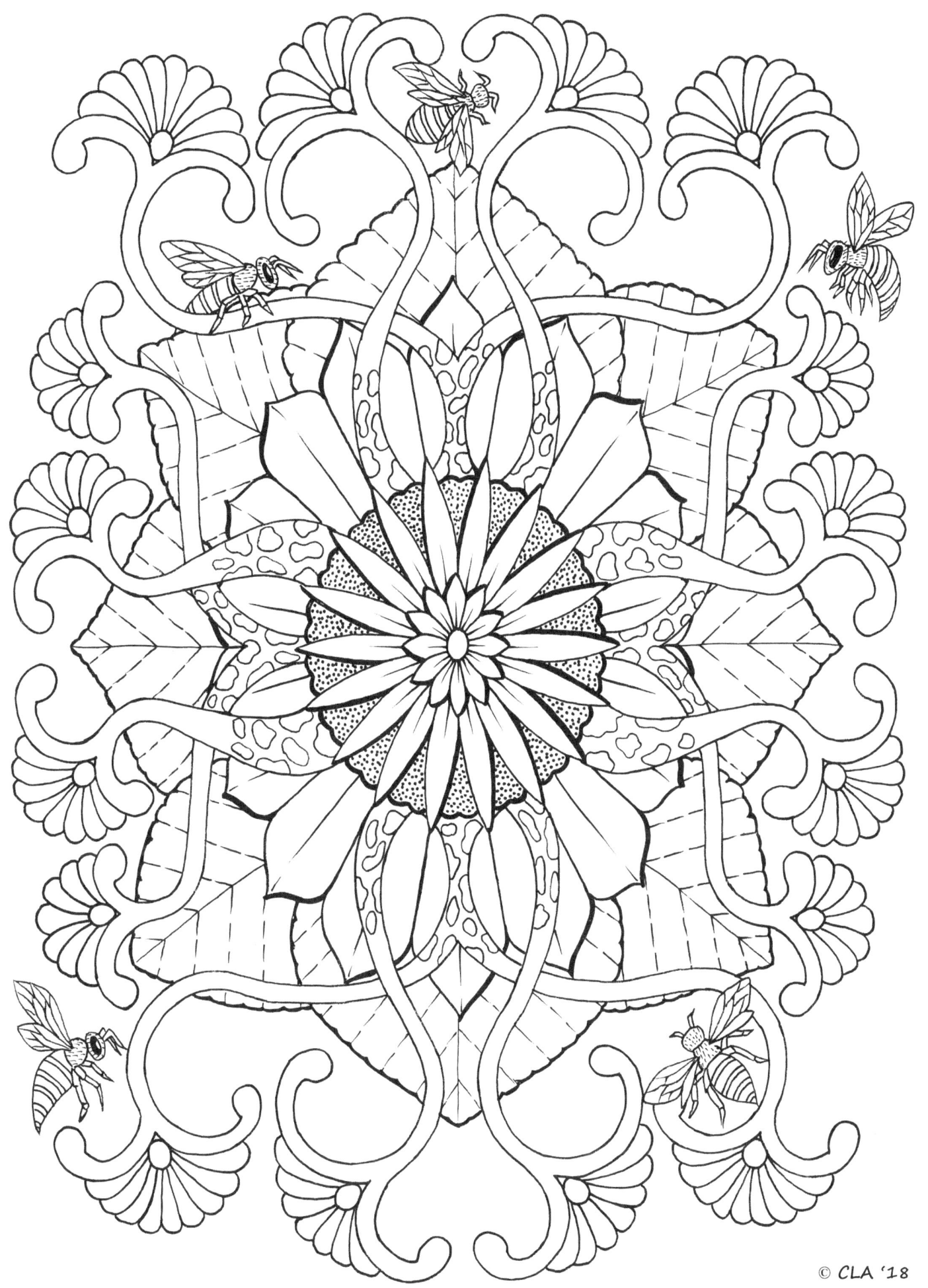

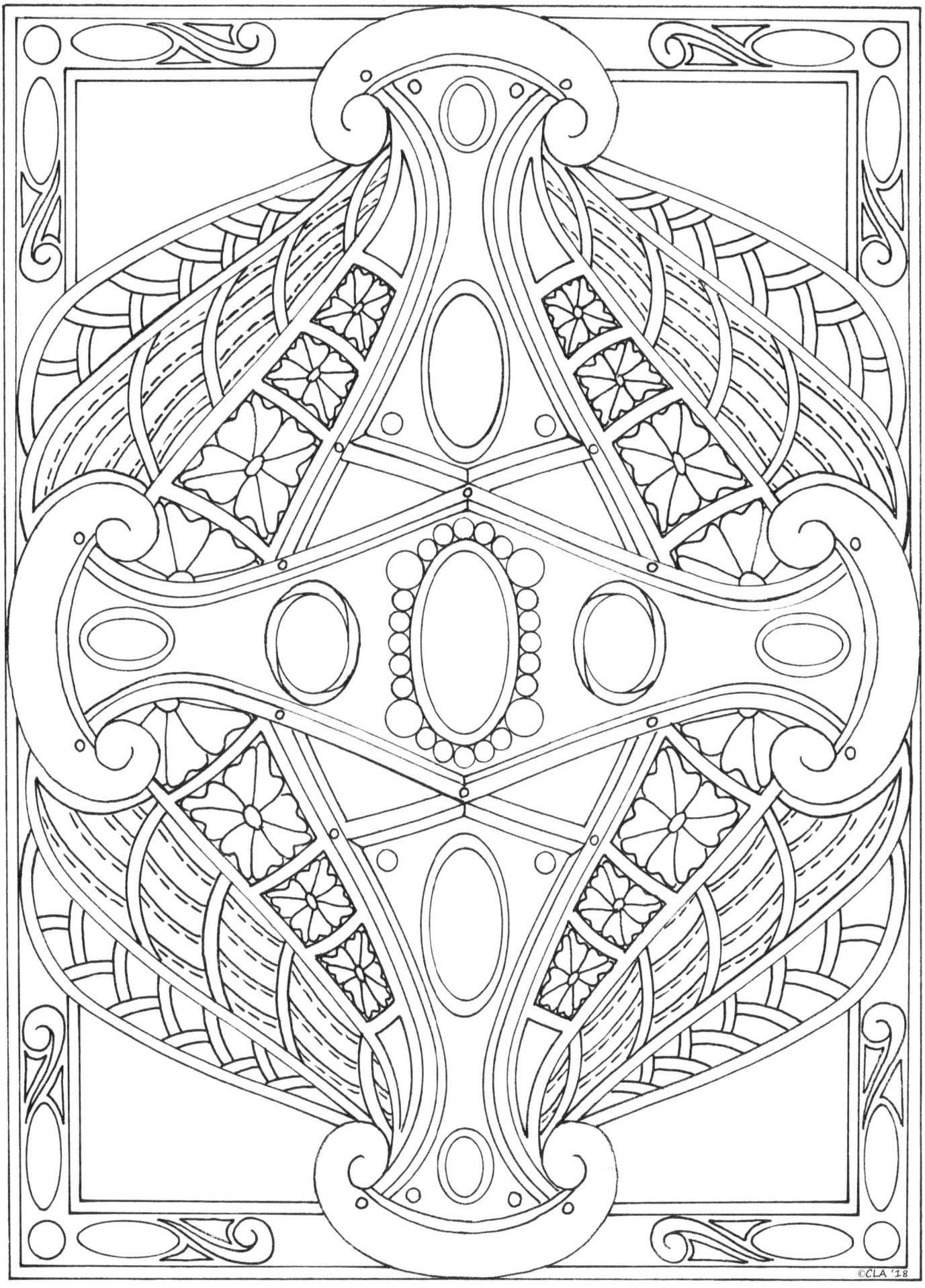

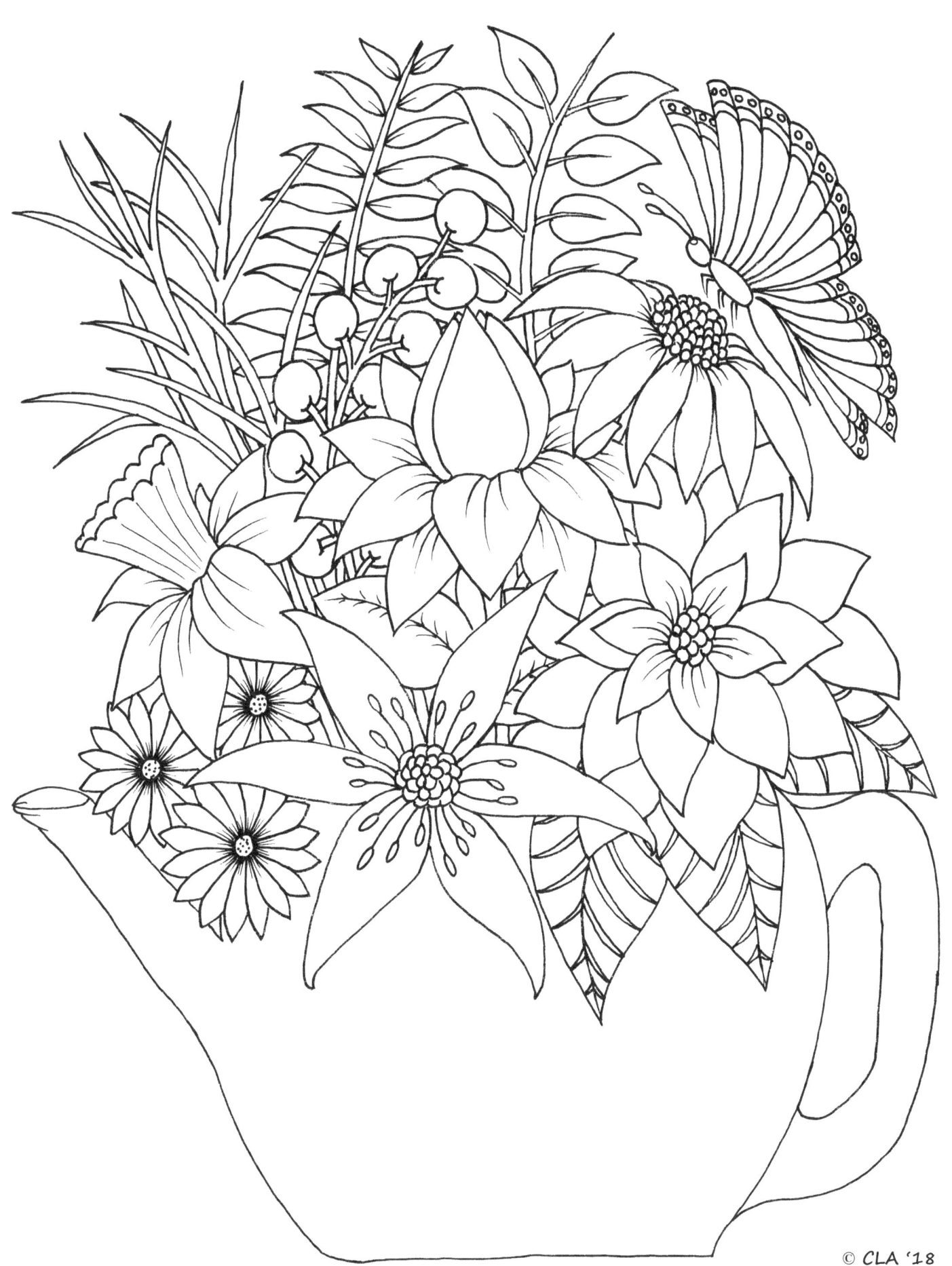

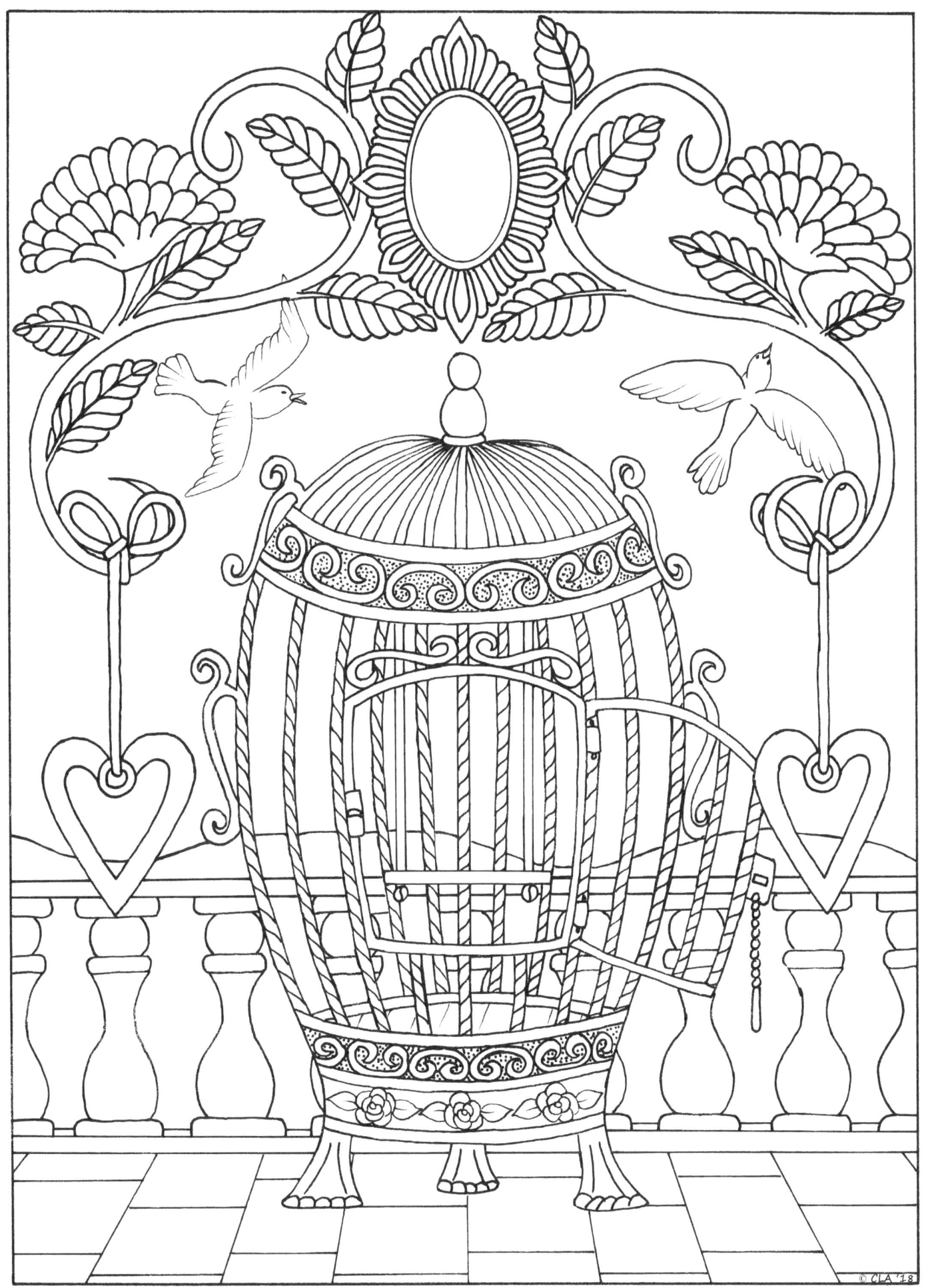

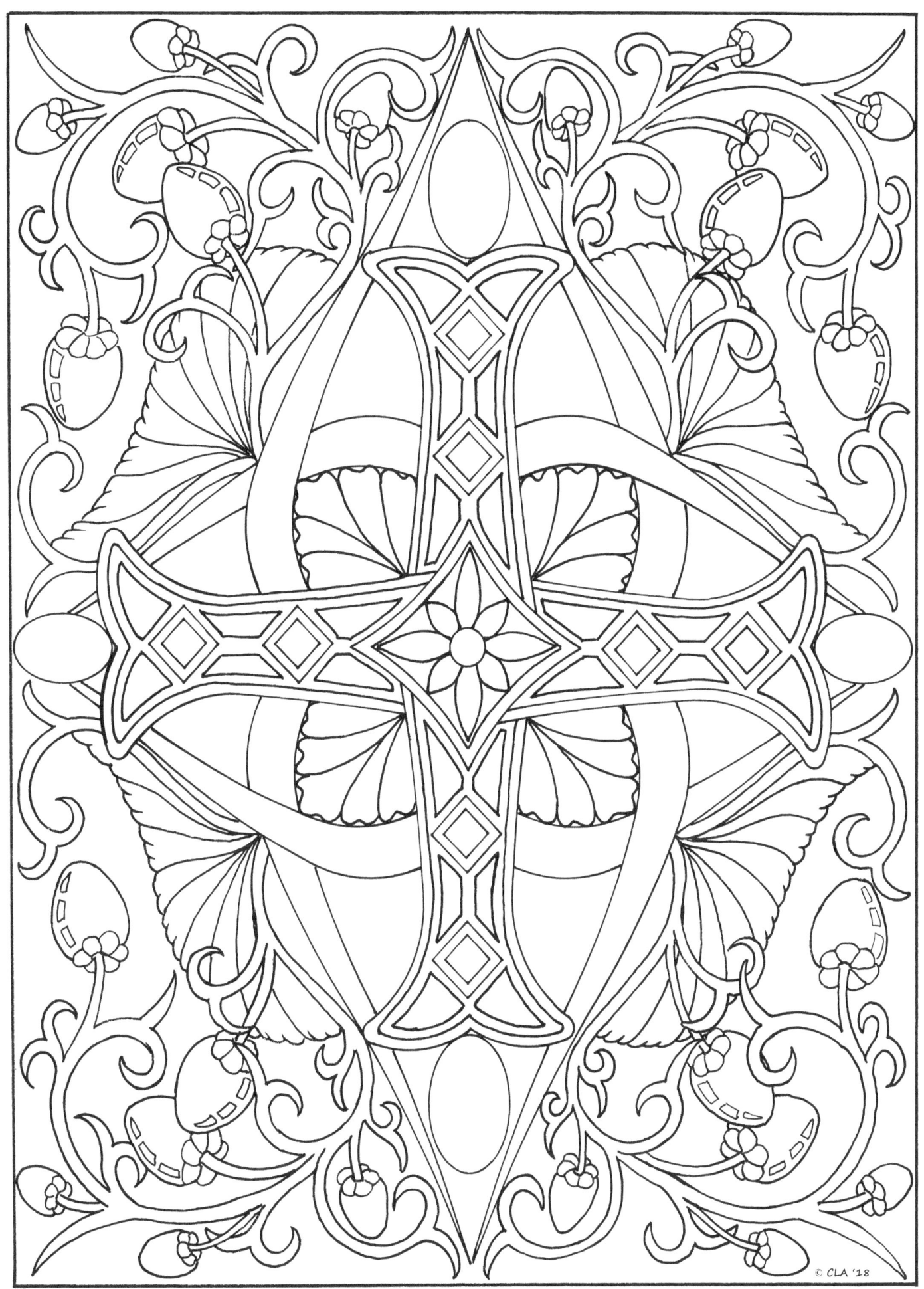

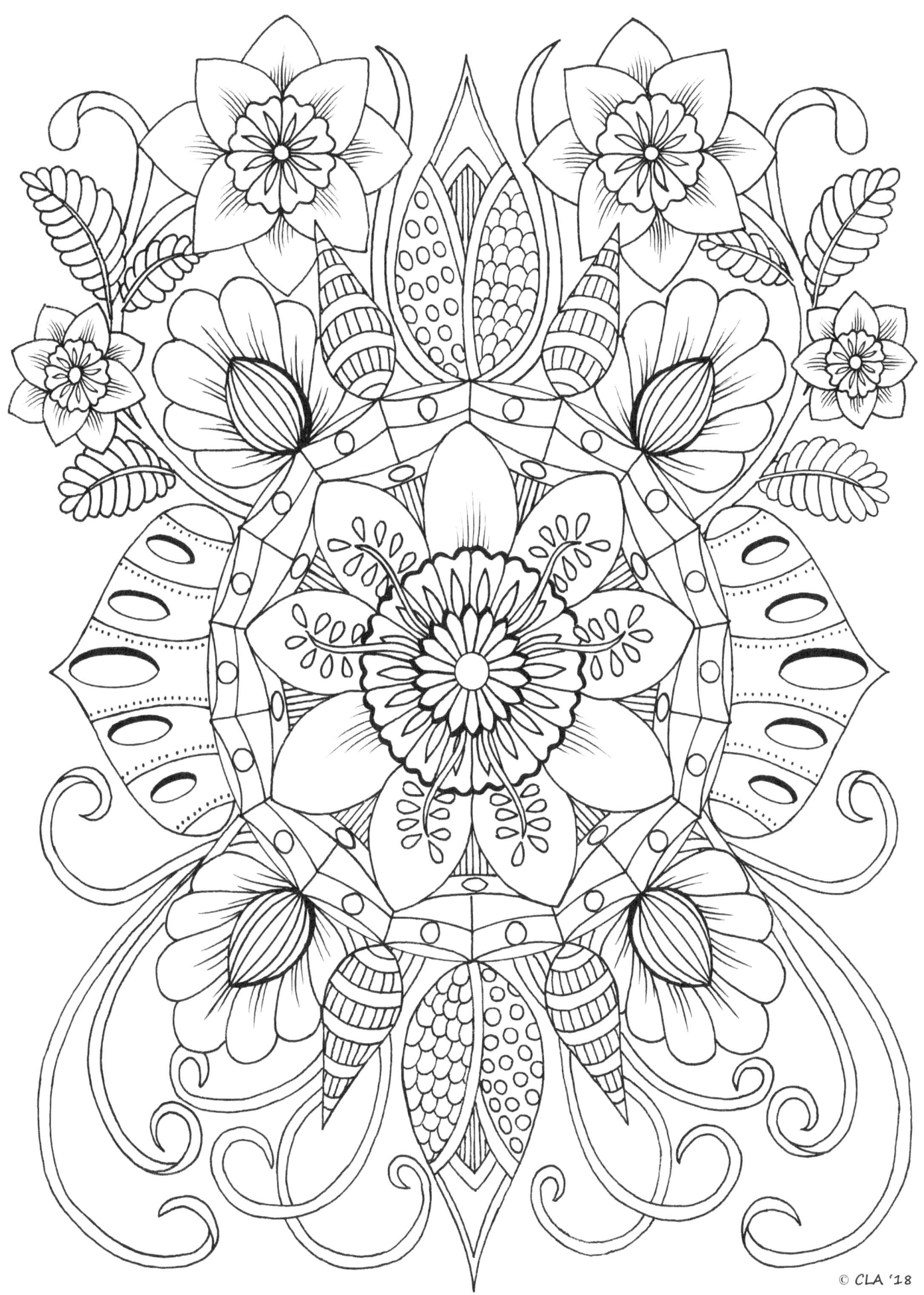

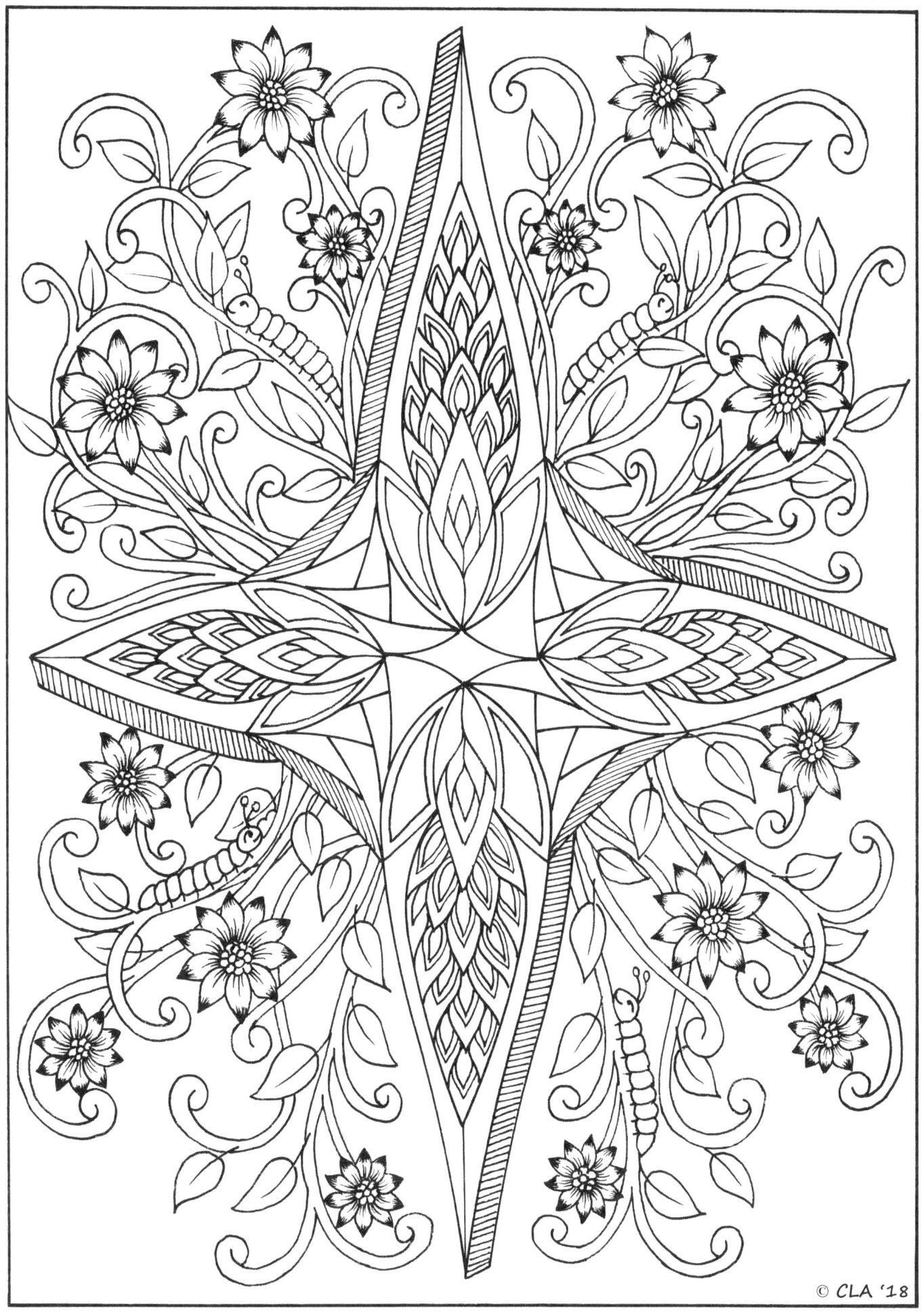

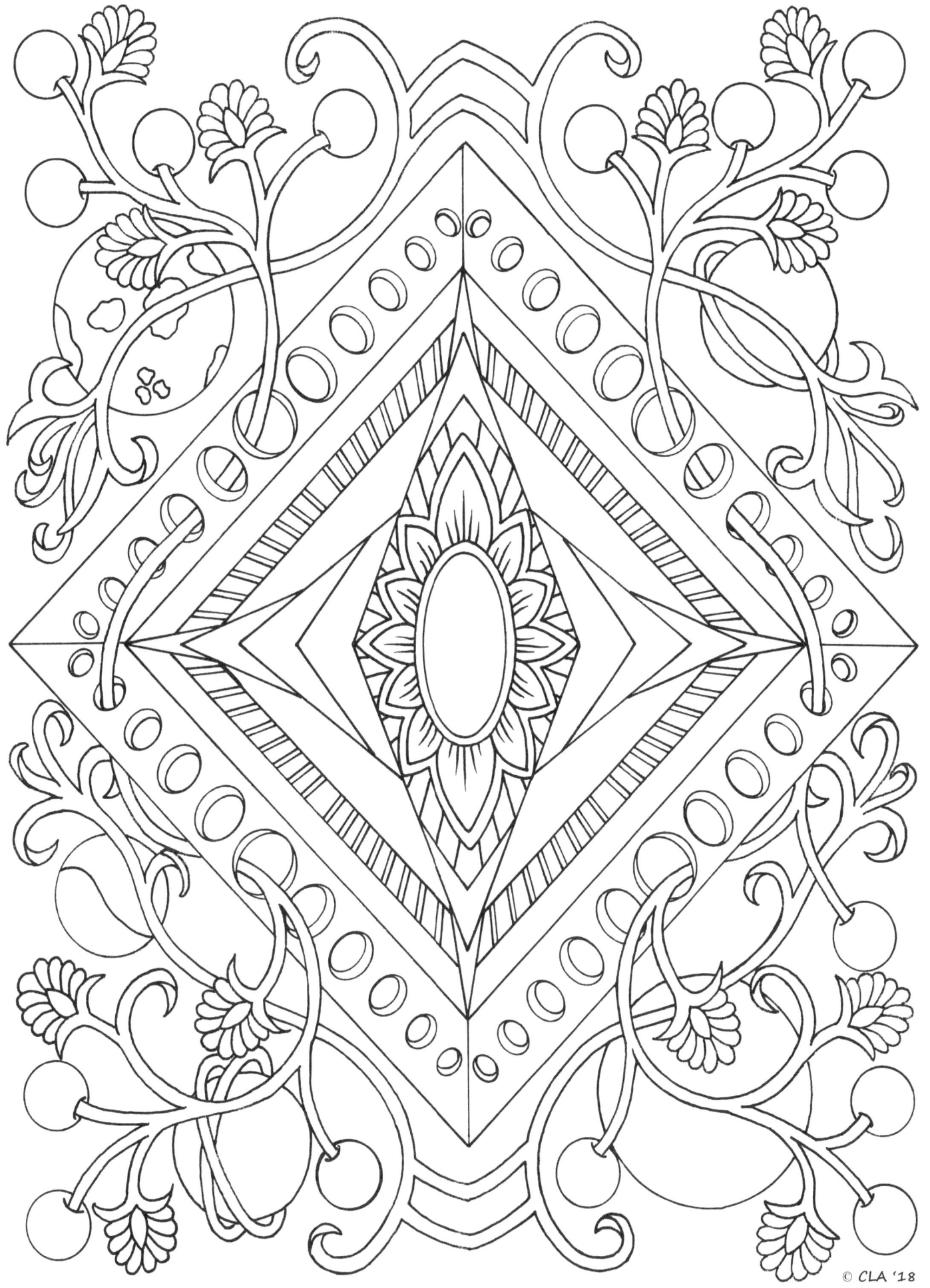

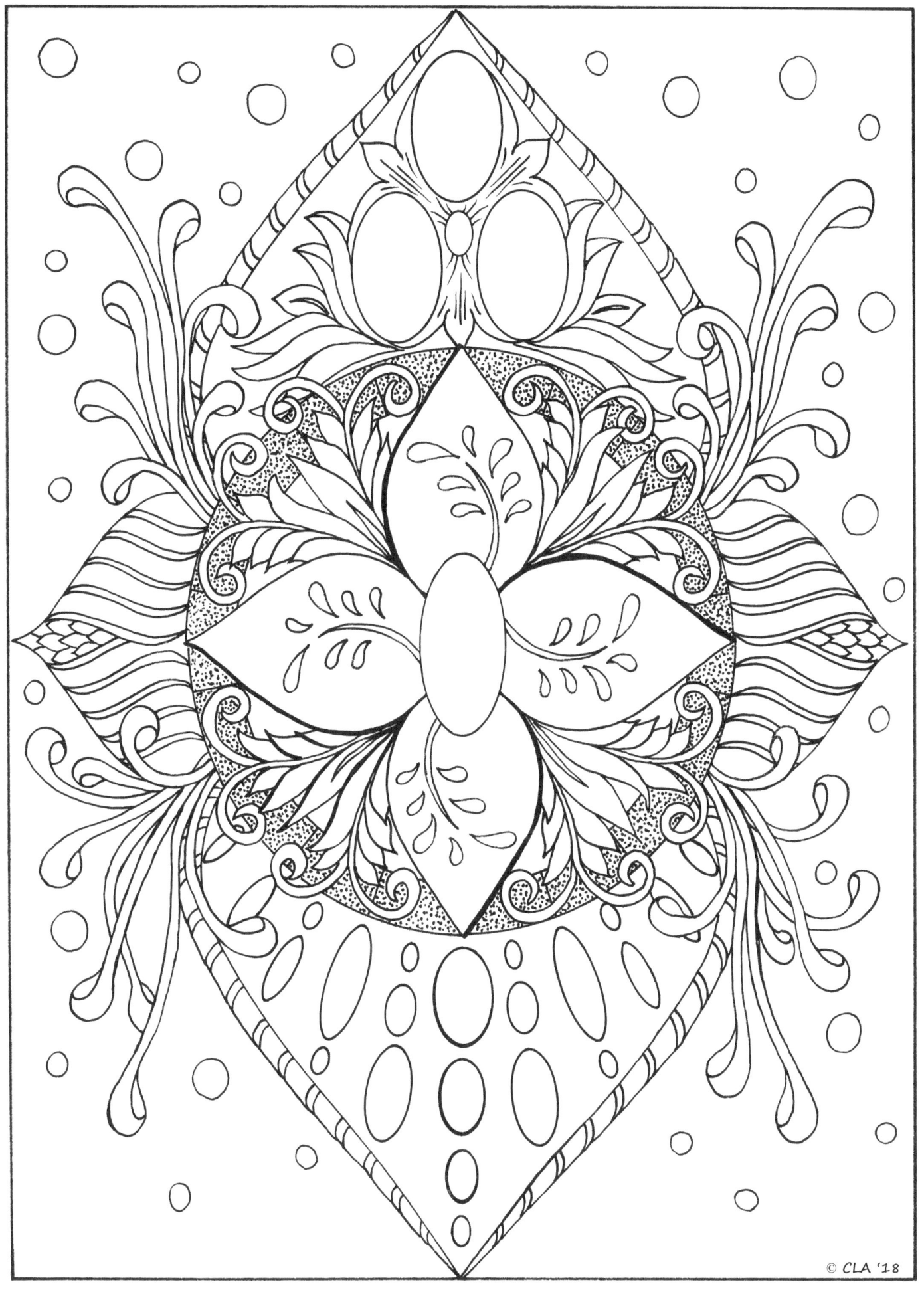

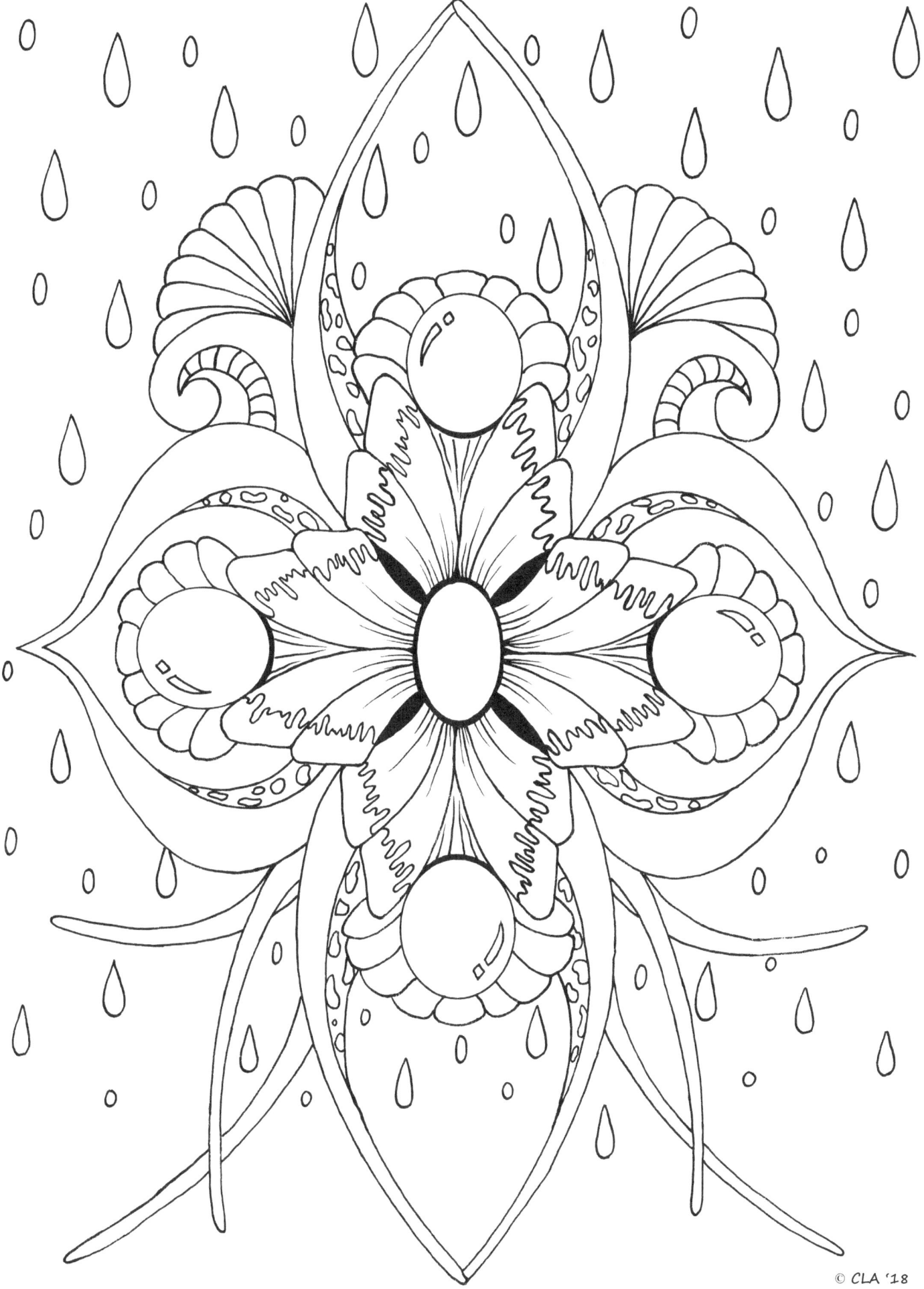

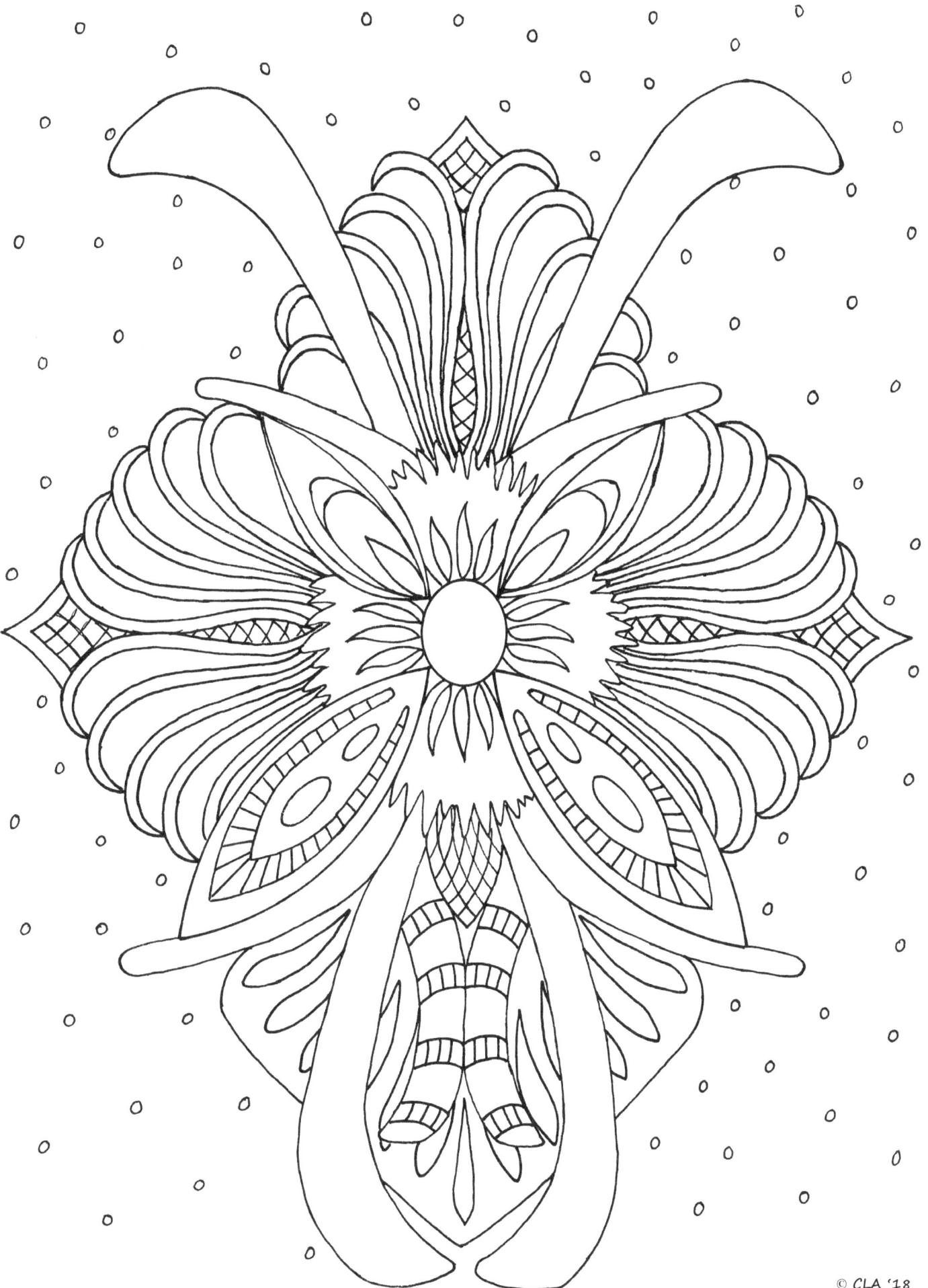

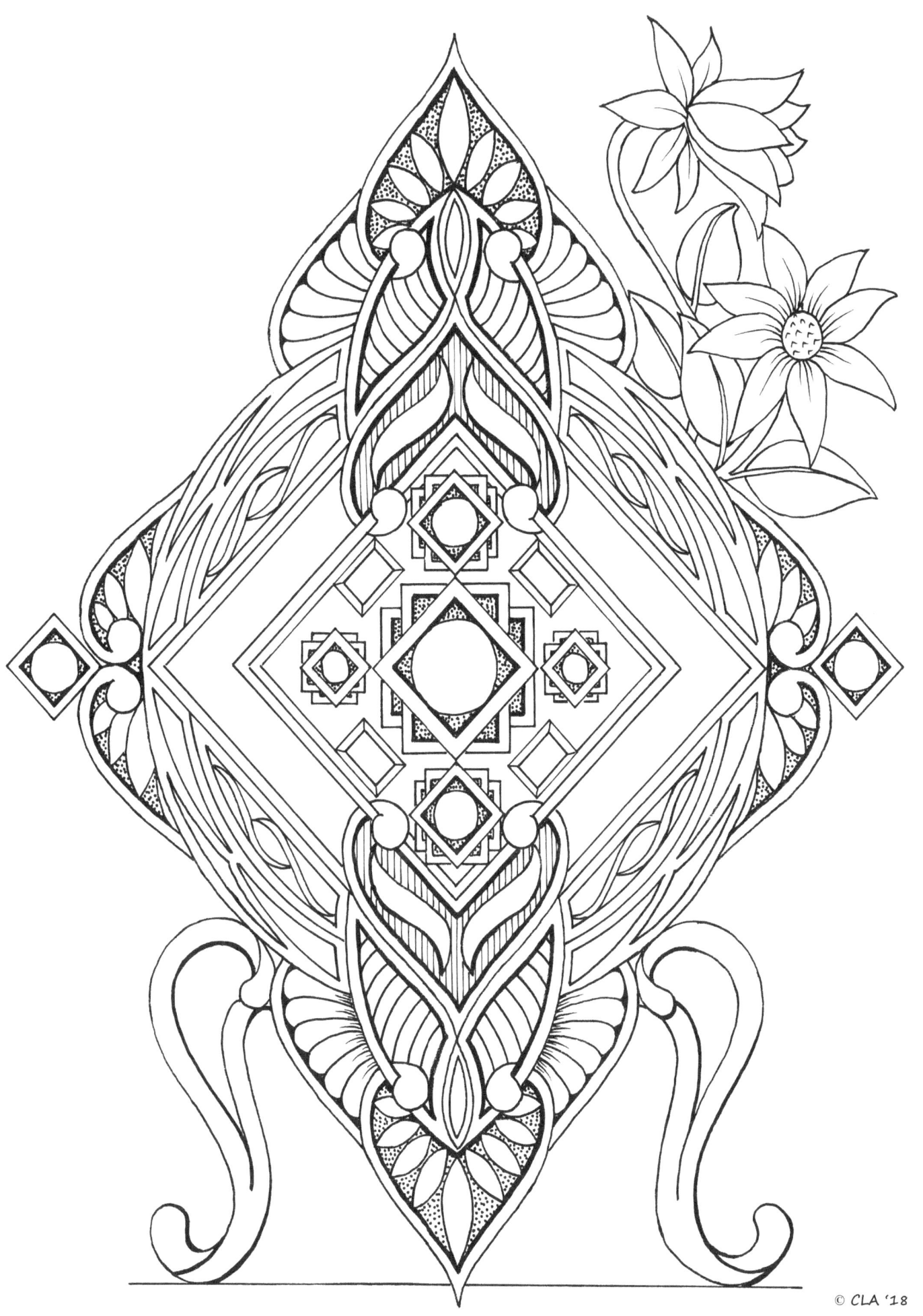

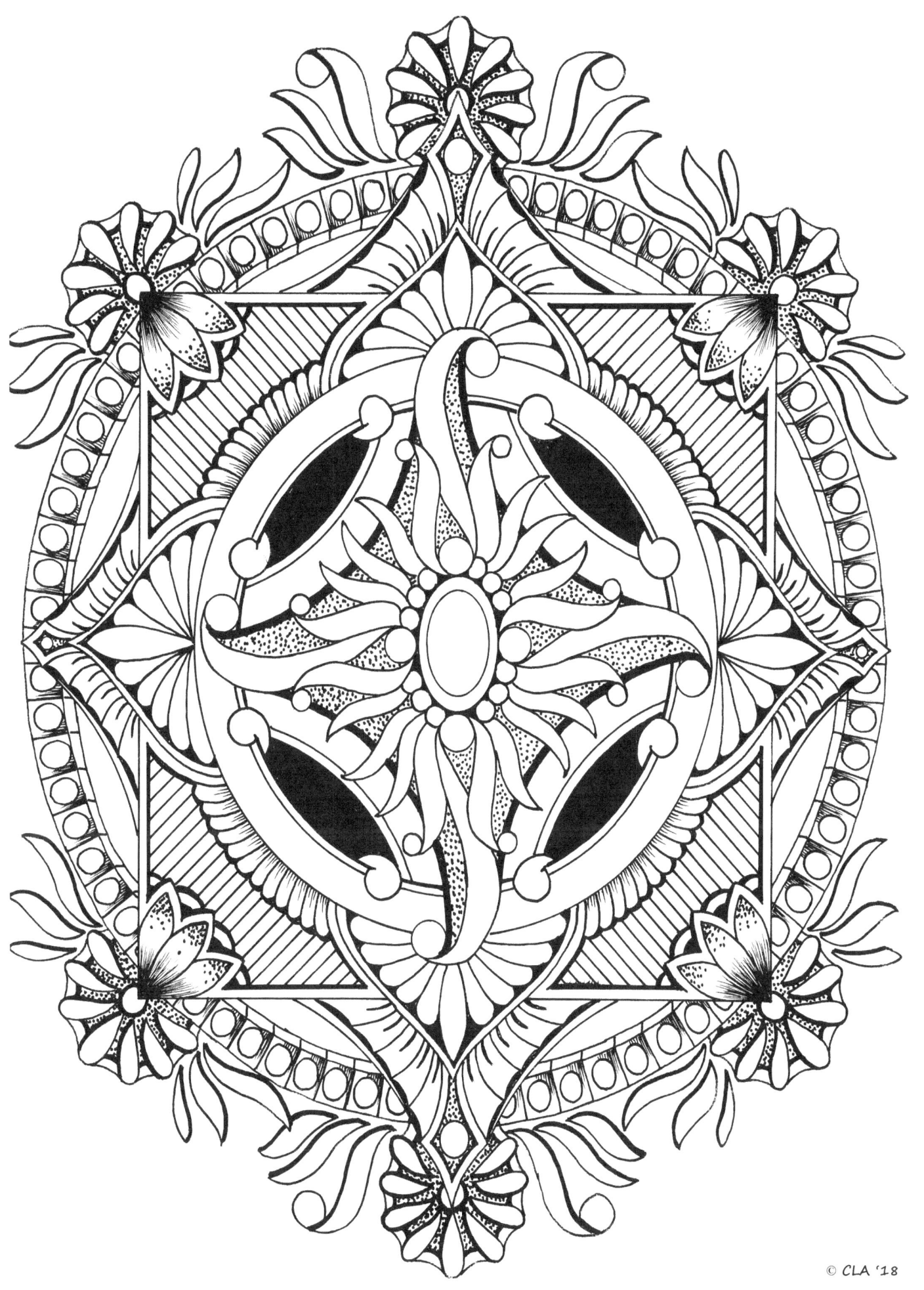

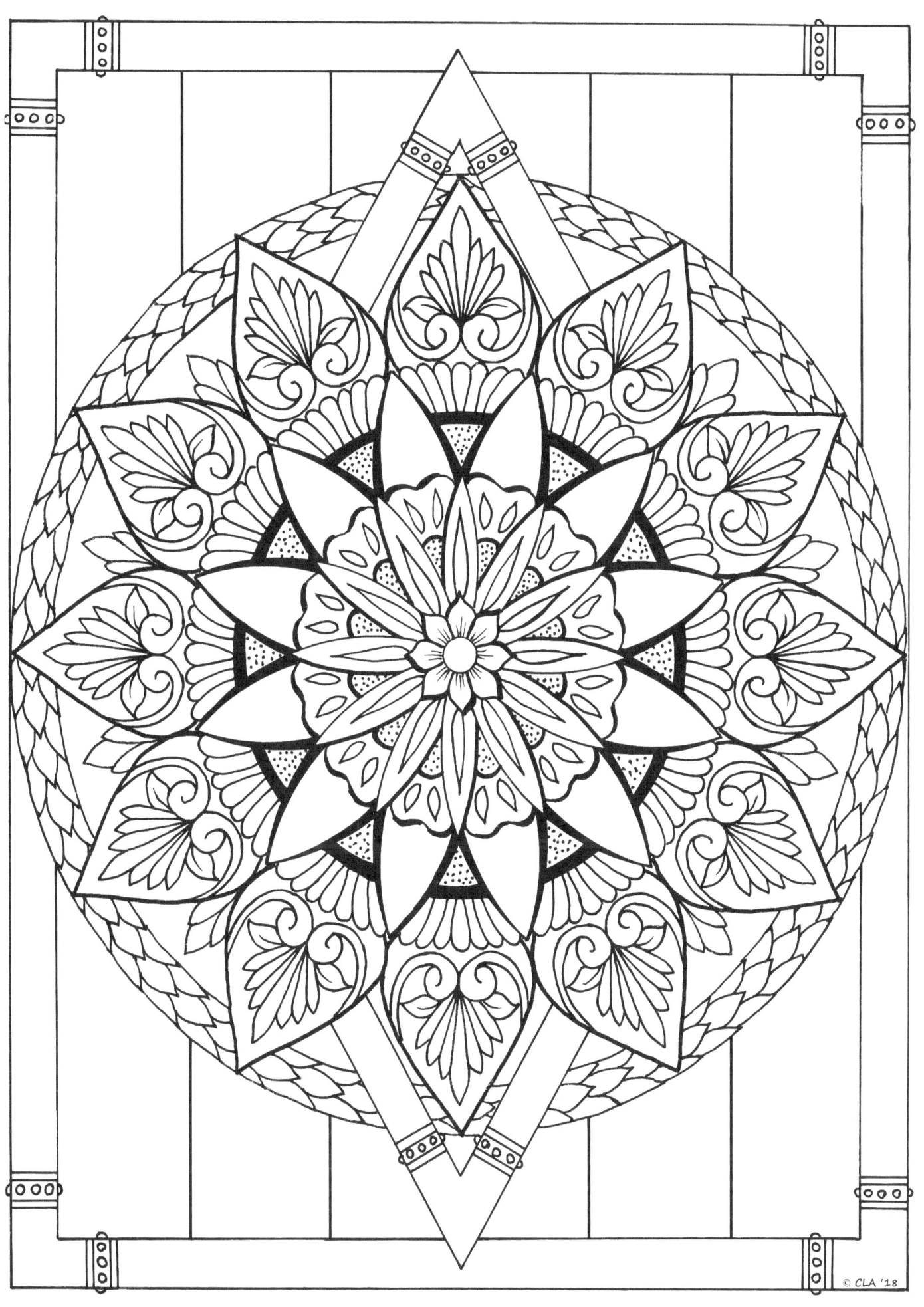

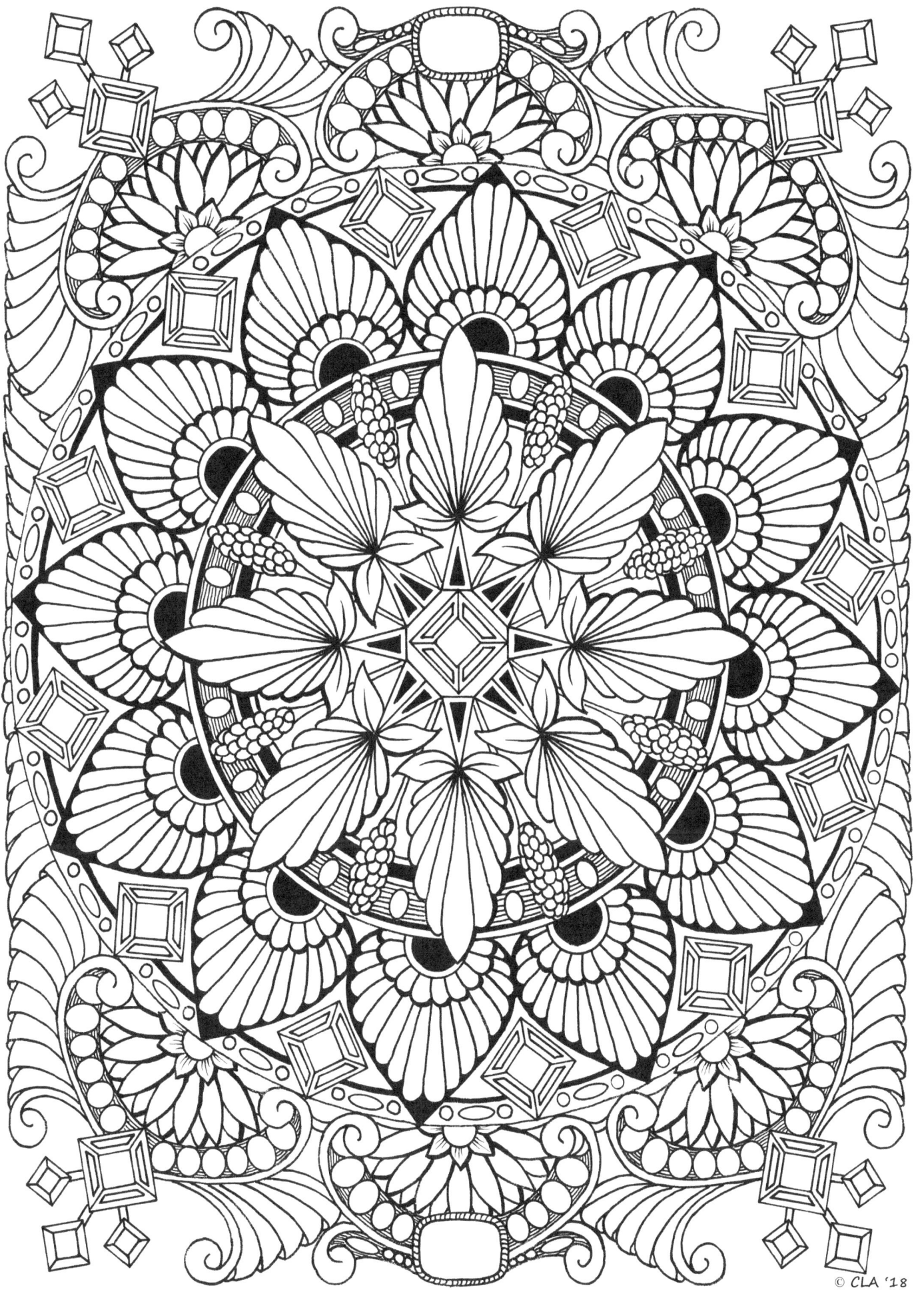

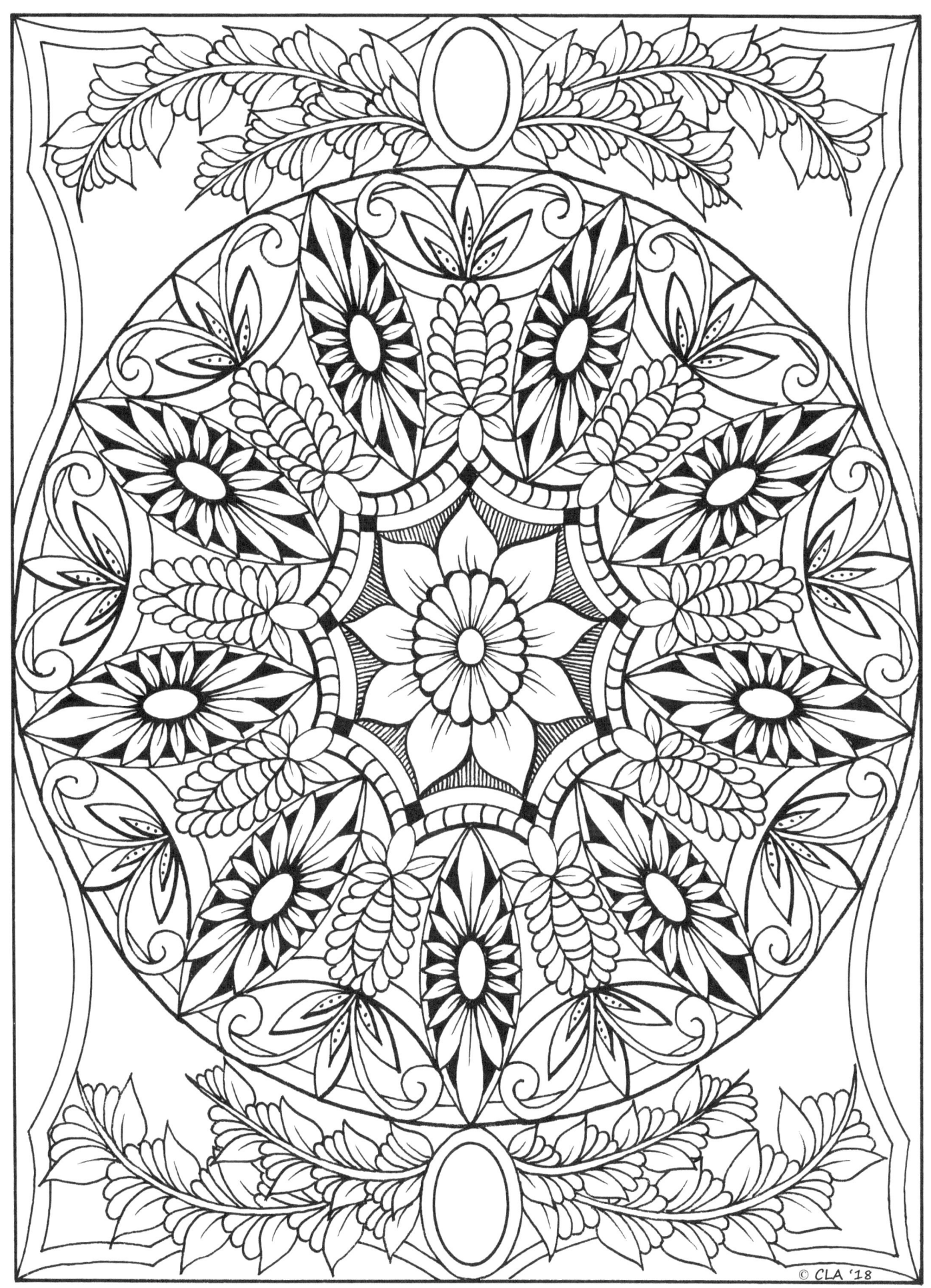

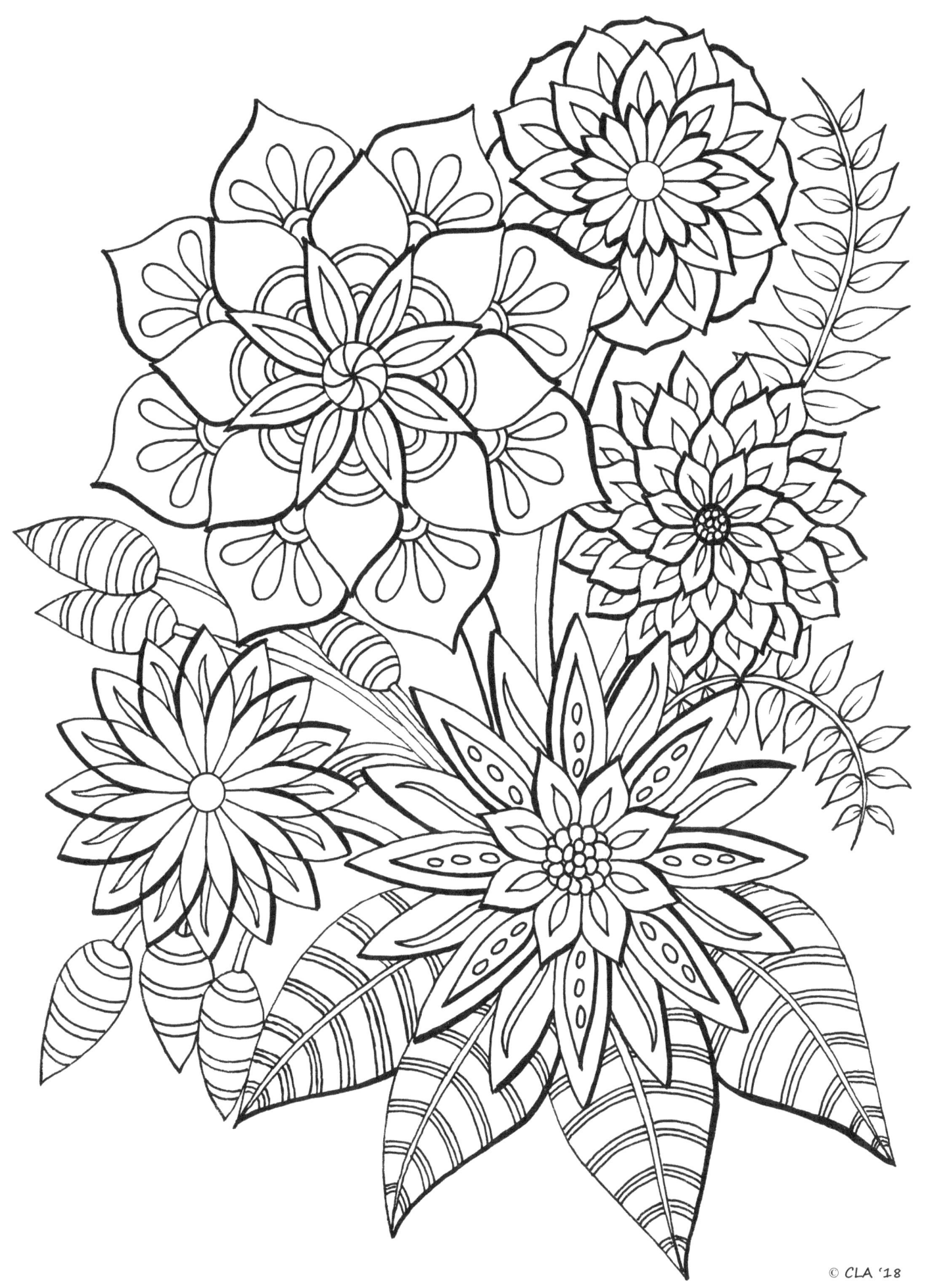

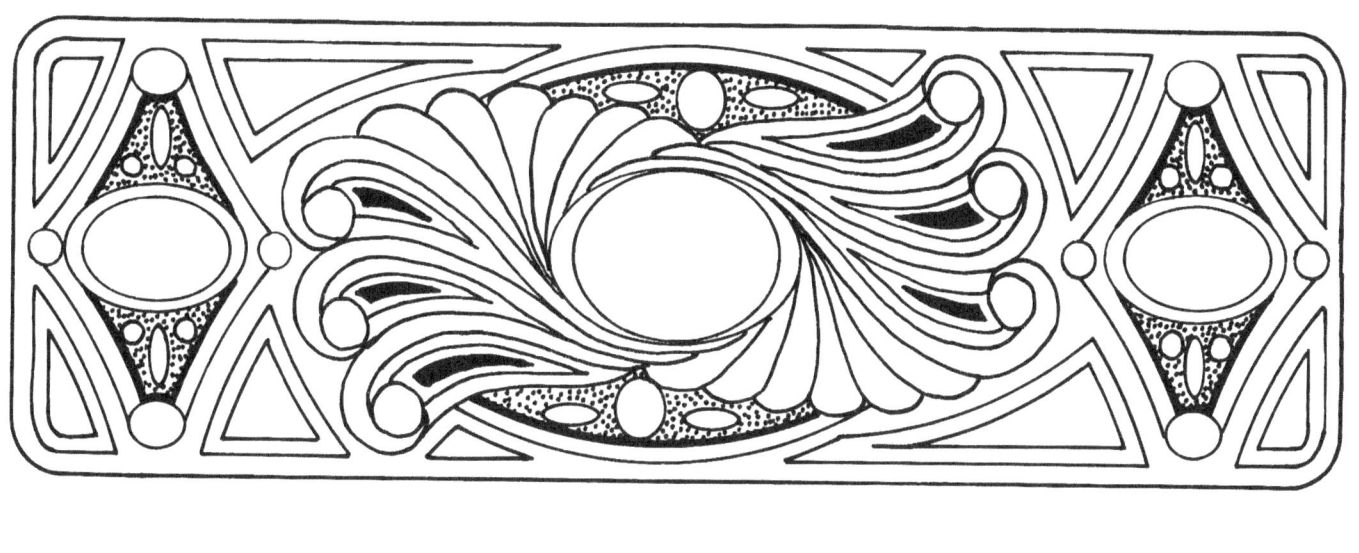
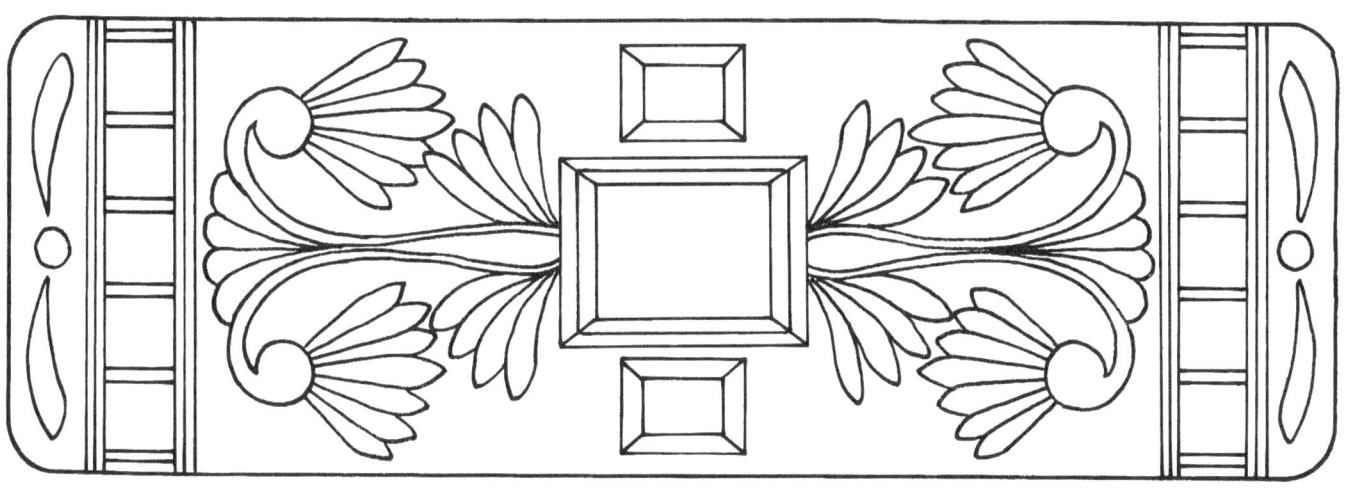
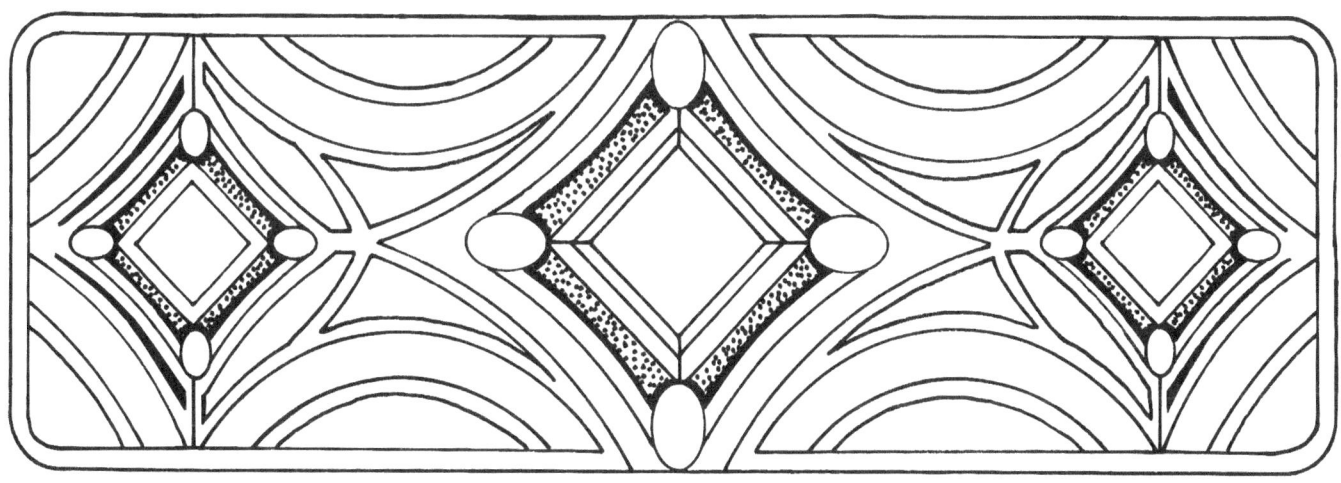

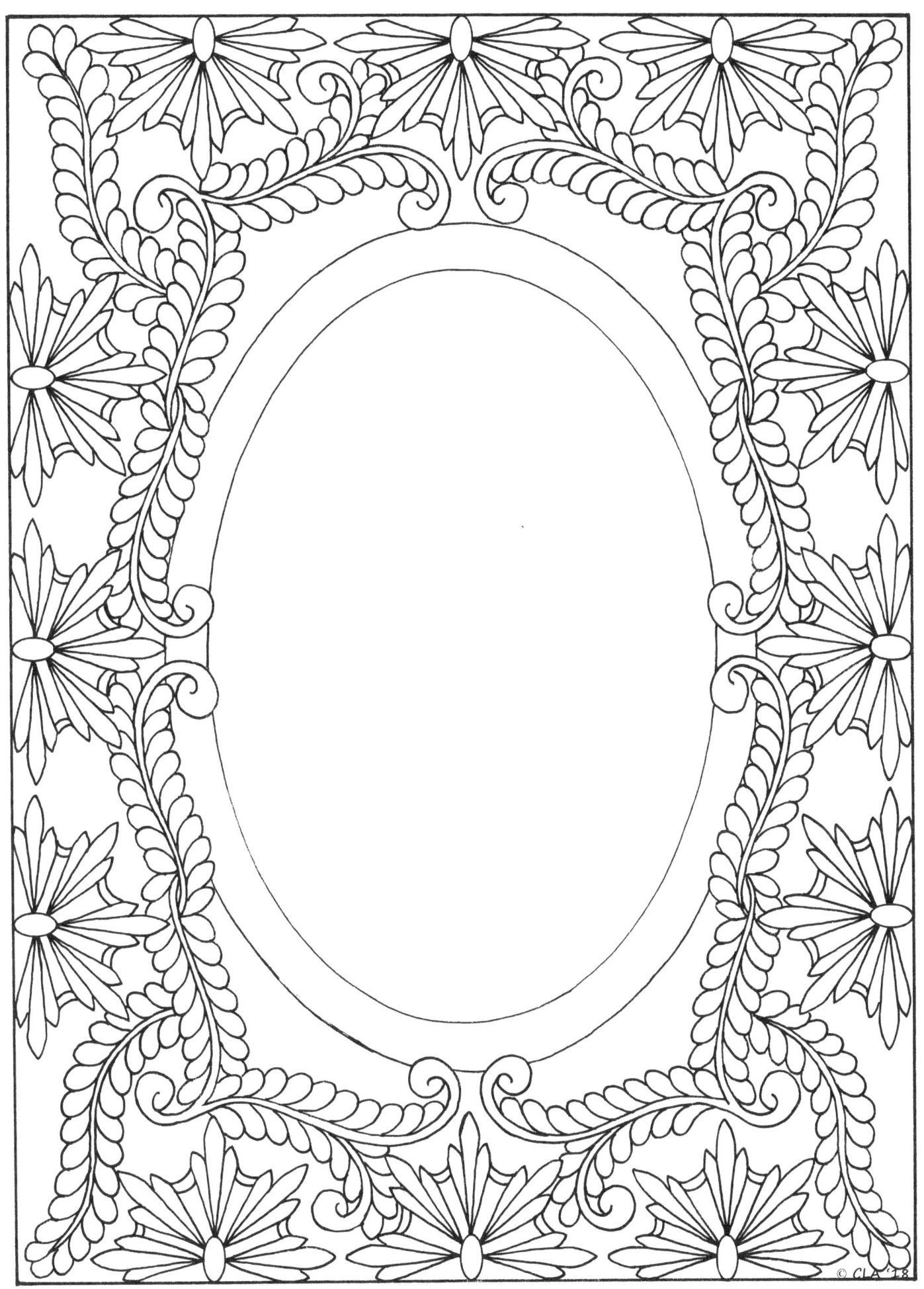

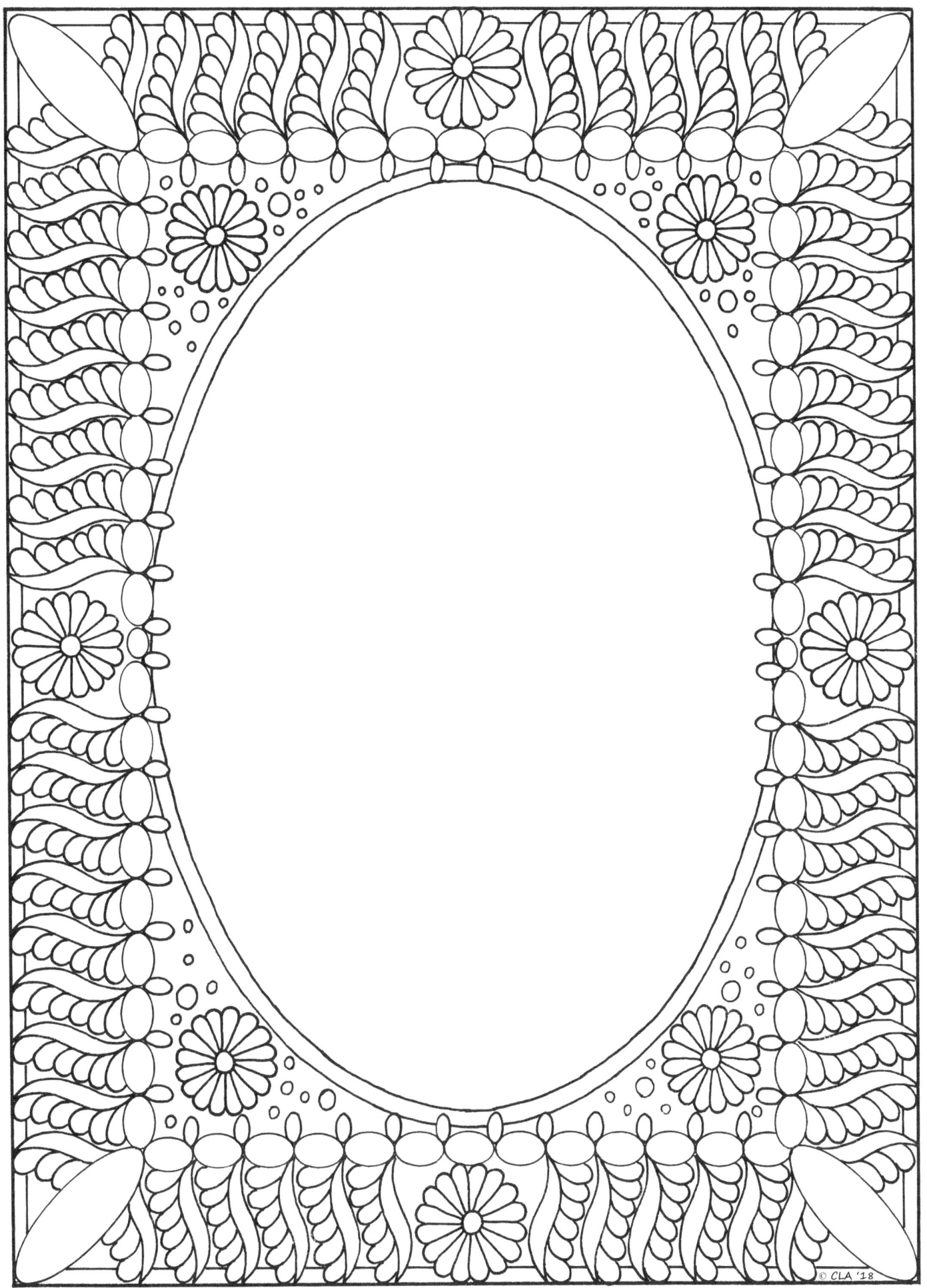

A FULL SET OF CRAFT/GREETING CARD BONUS PAGES

Adapted versions of the larger drawings, perfect for framing (5" x 7"), or for crafting, scrapbooking, and making greeting cards!

Also great for working out your color schemes for the larger drawings.

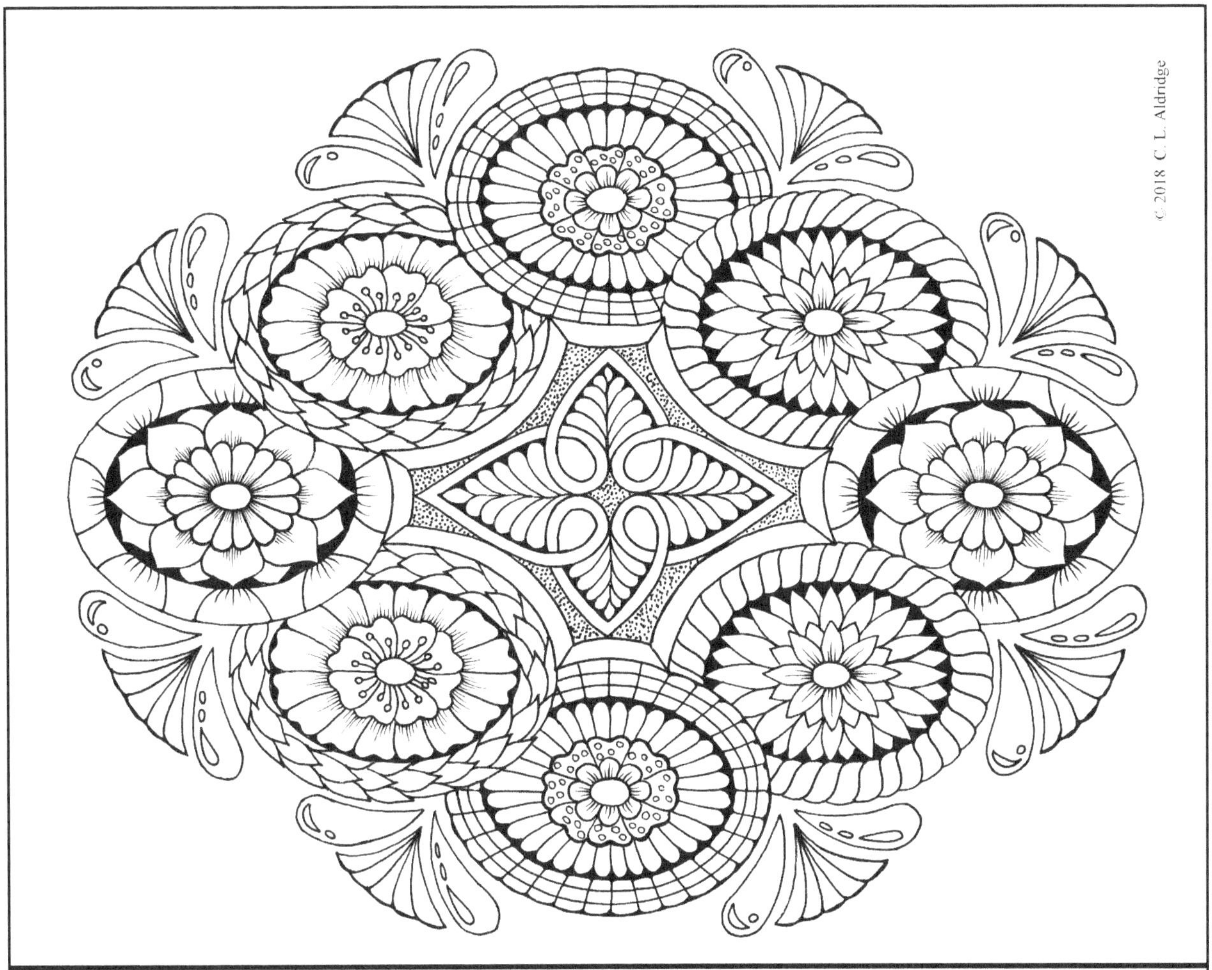

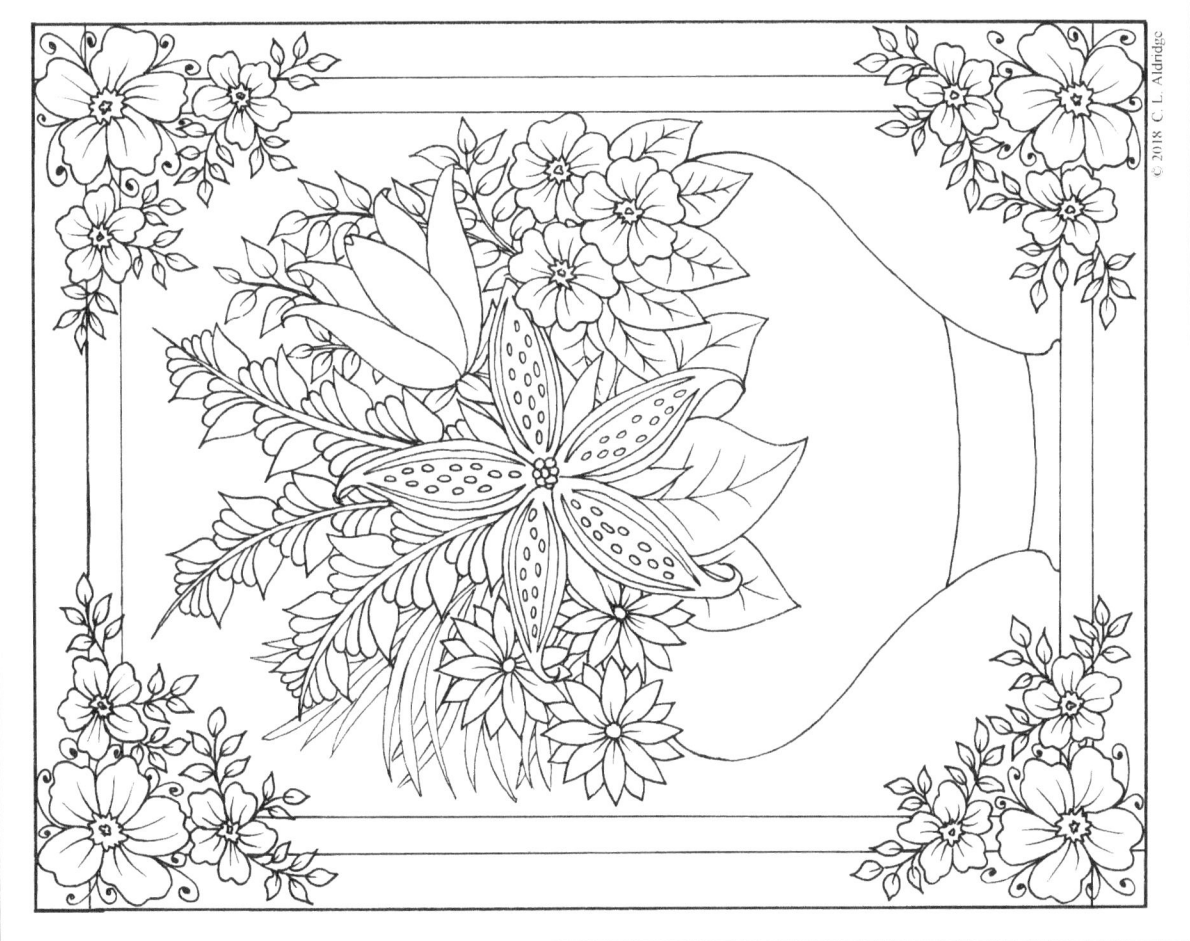

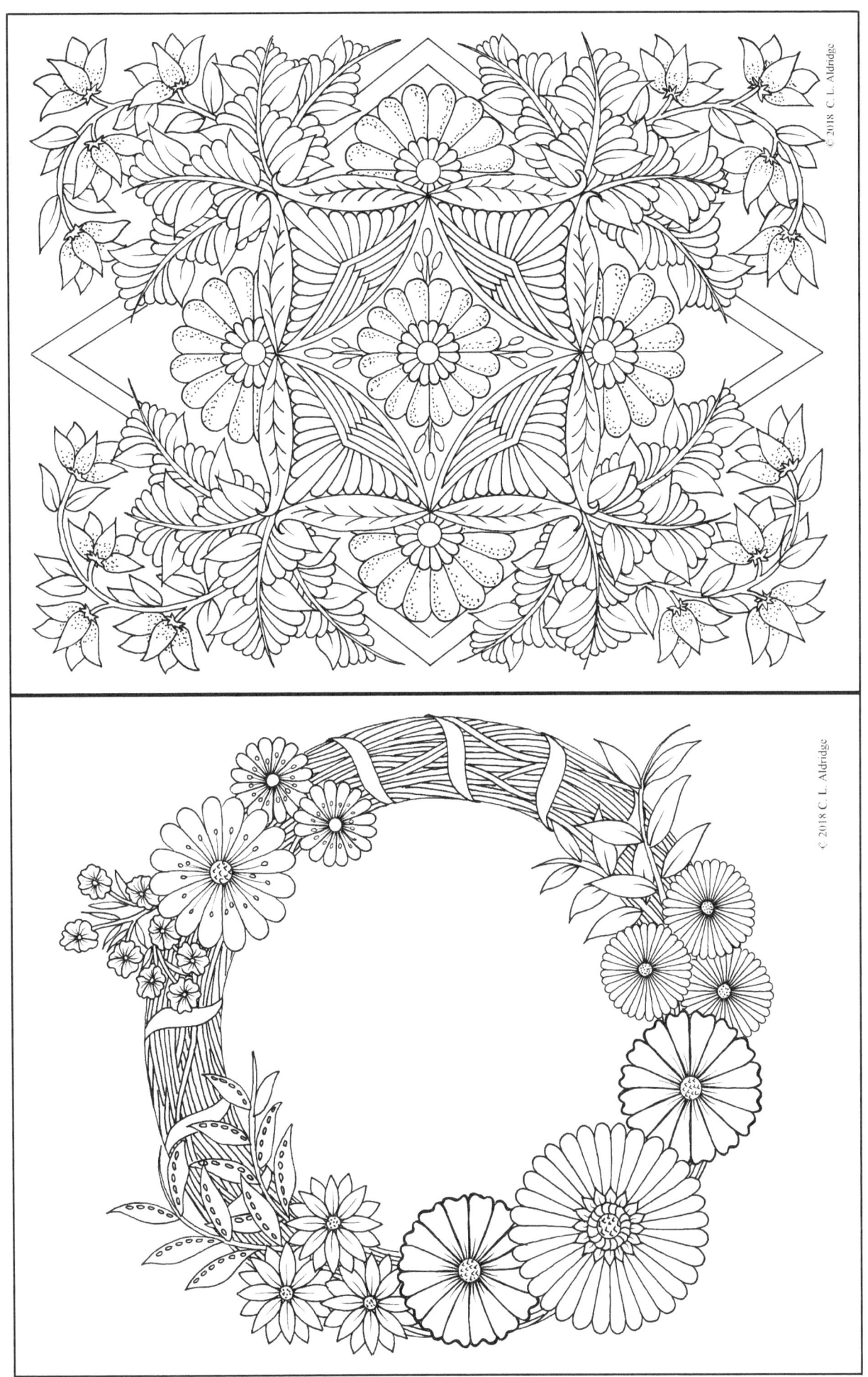

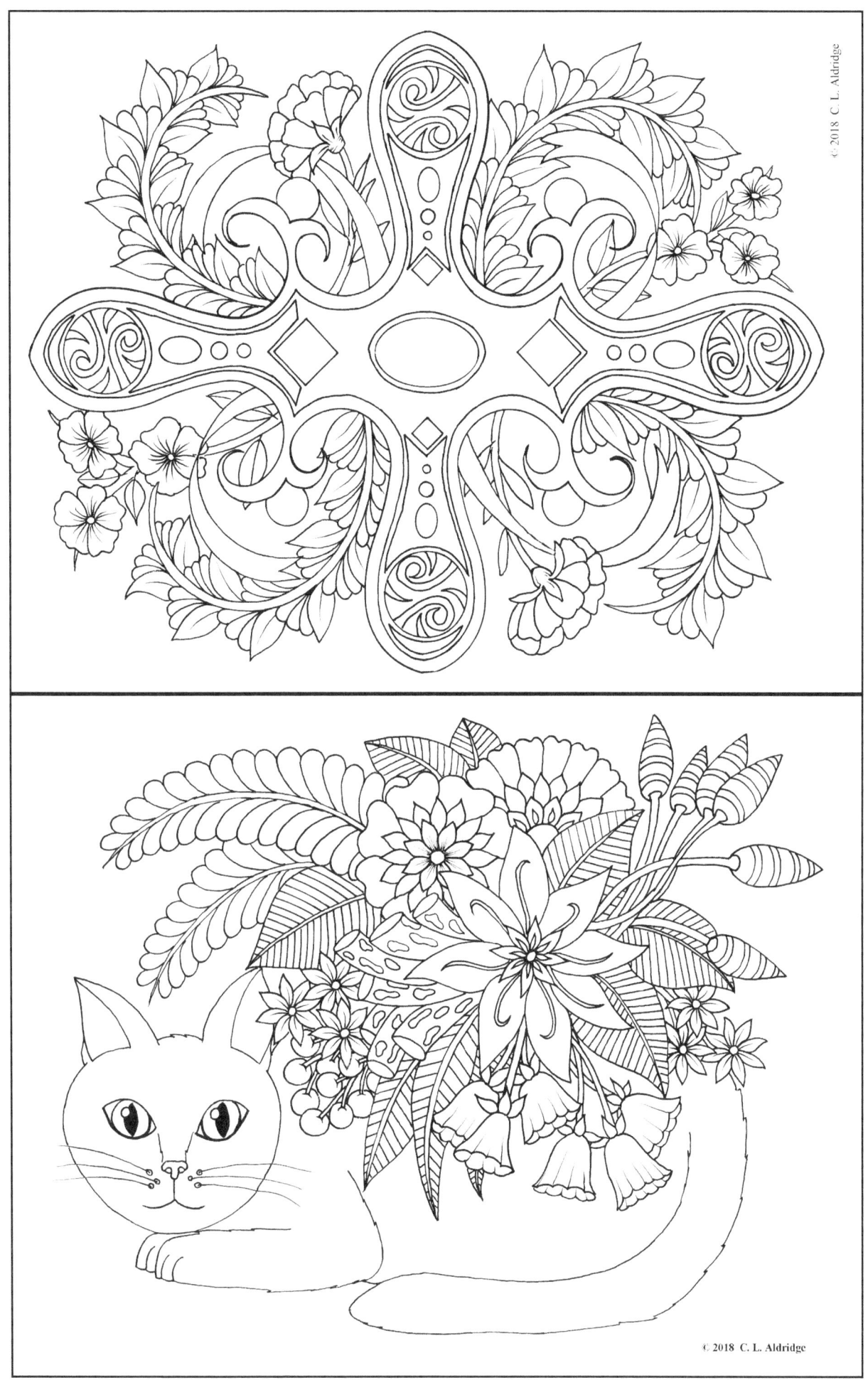

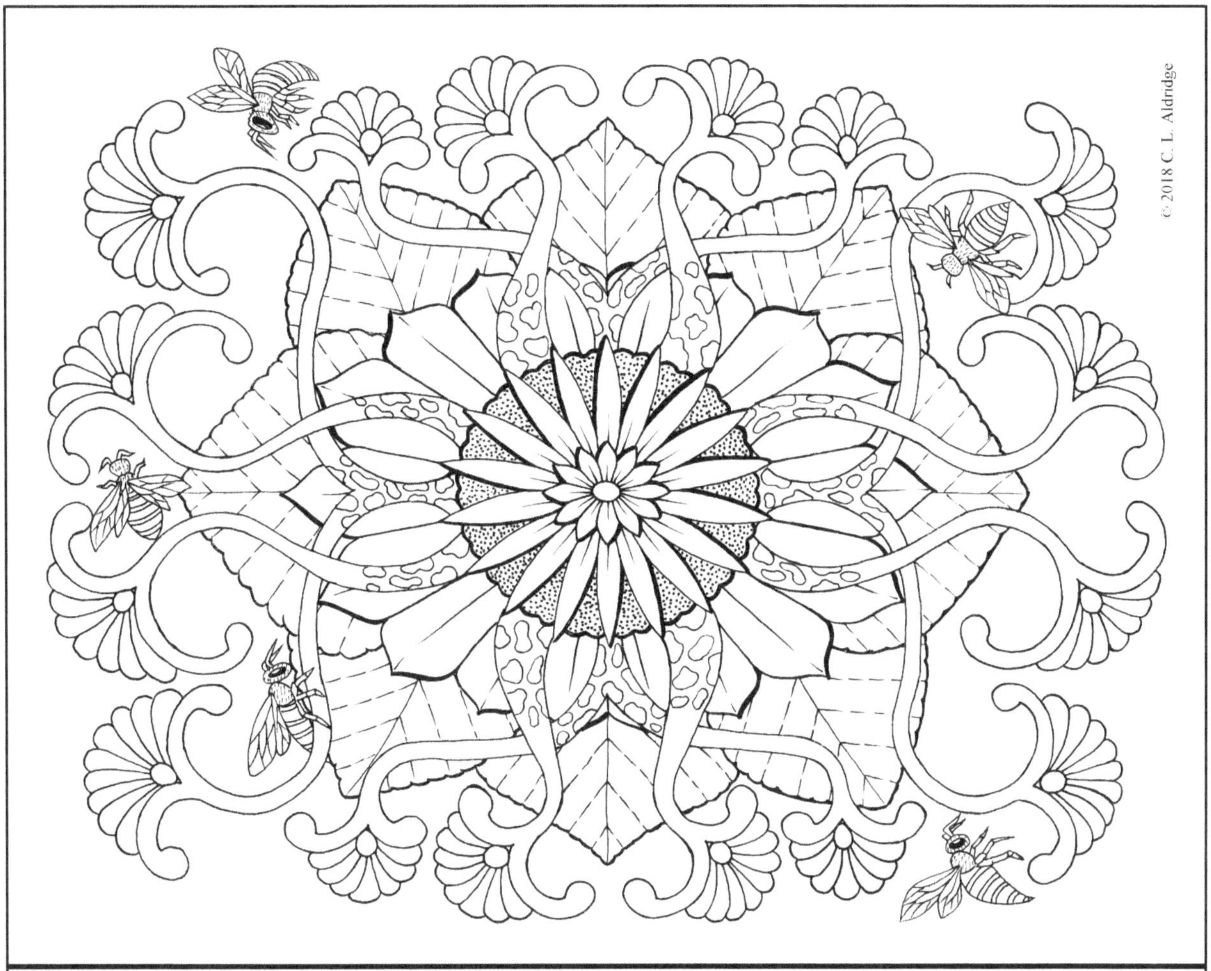

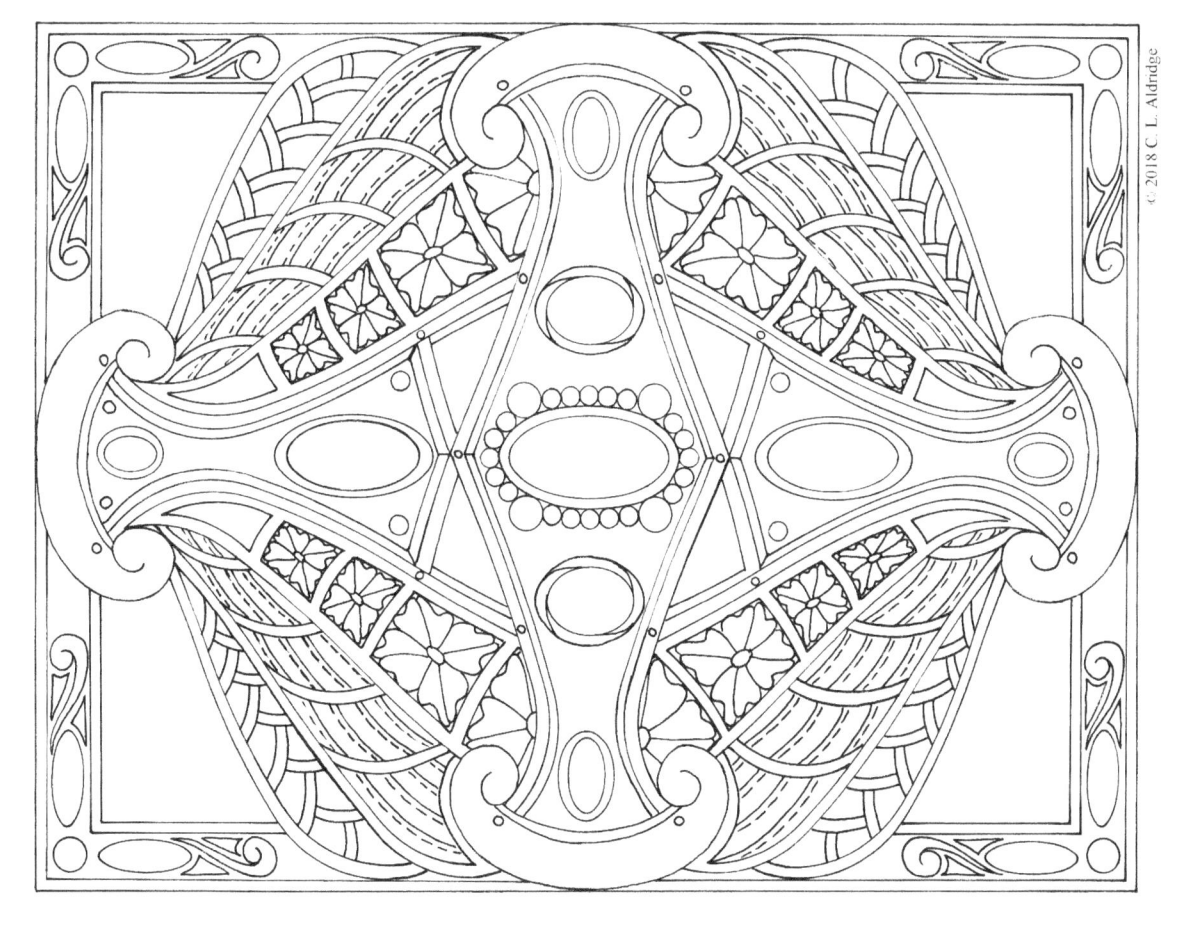

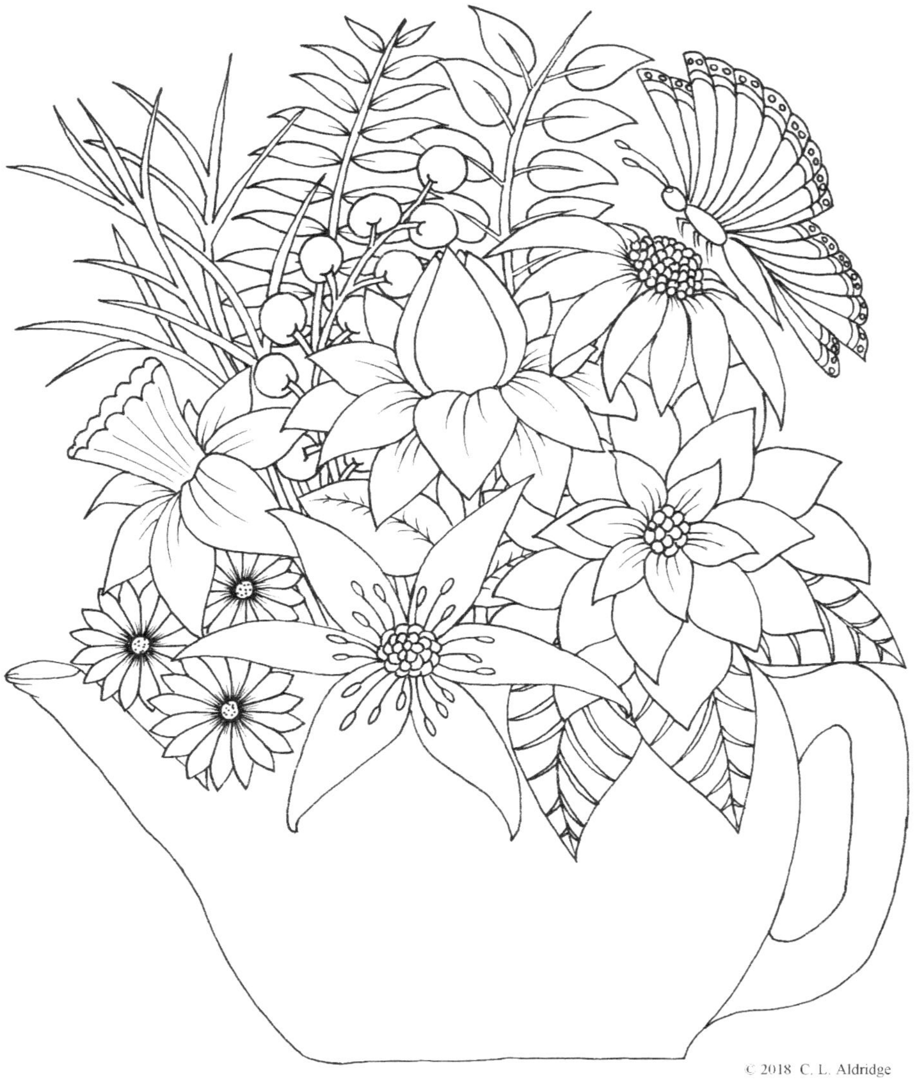

© 2018 C. L. Aldridge

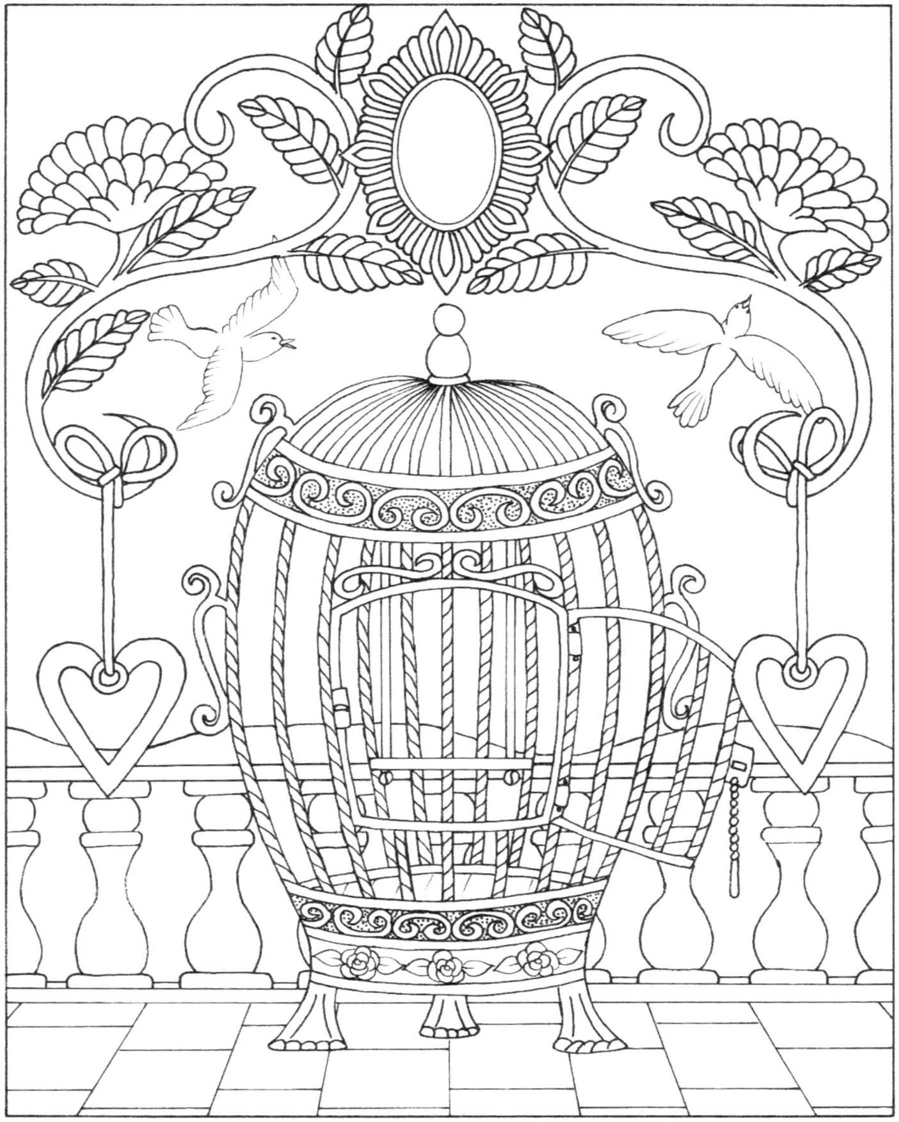

© 2018 C. L. Aldridge

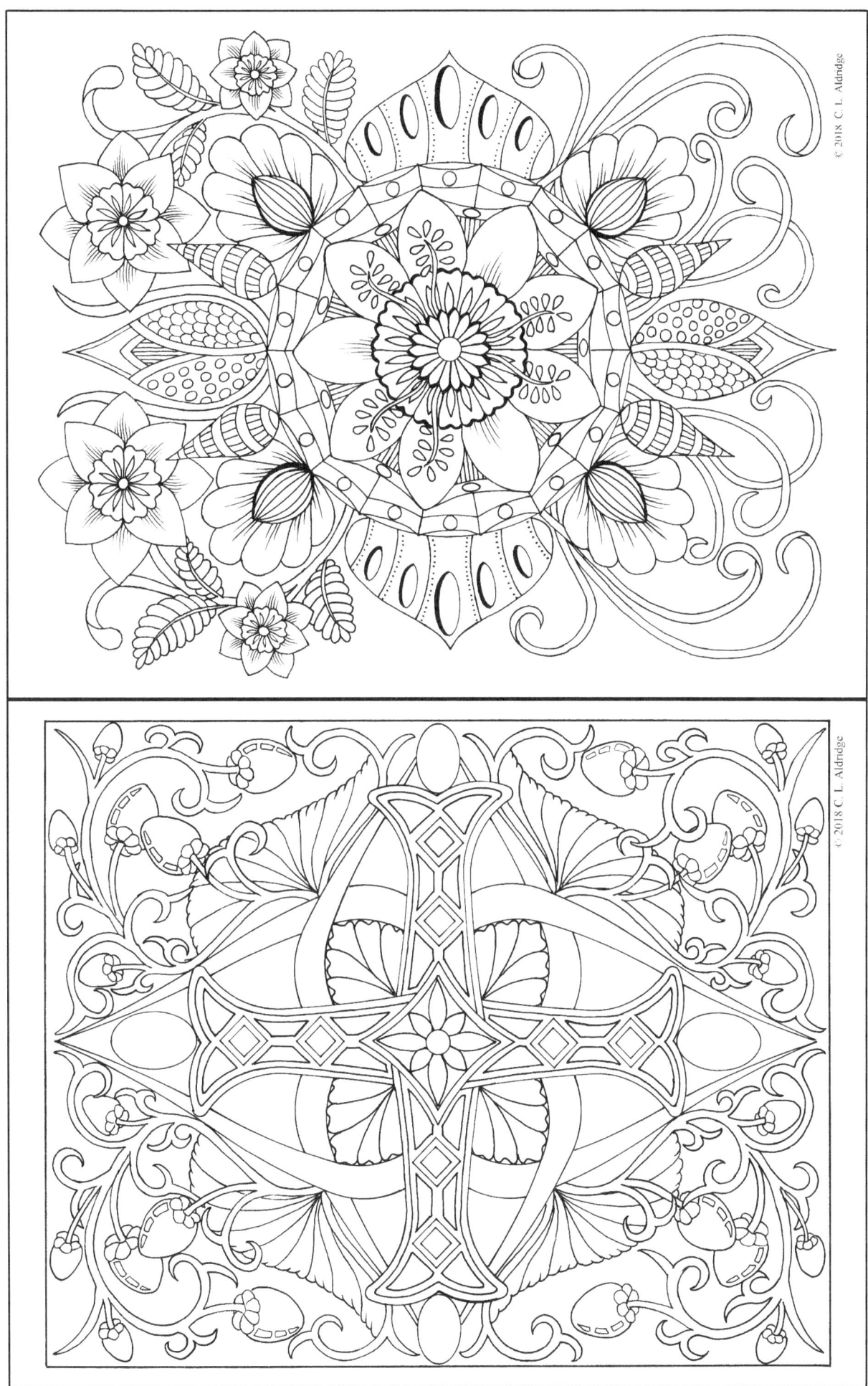

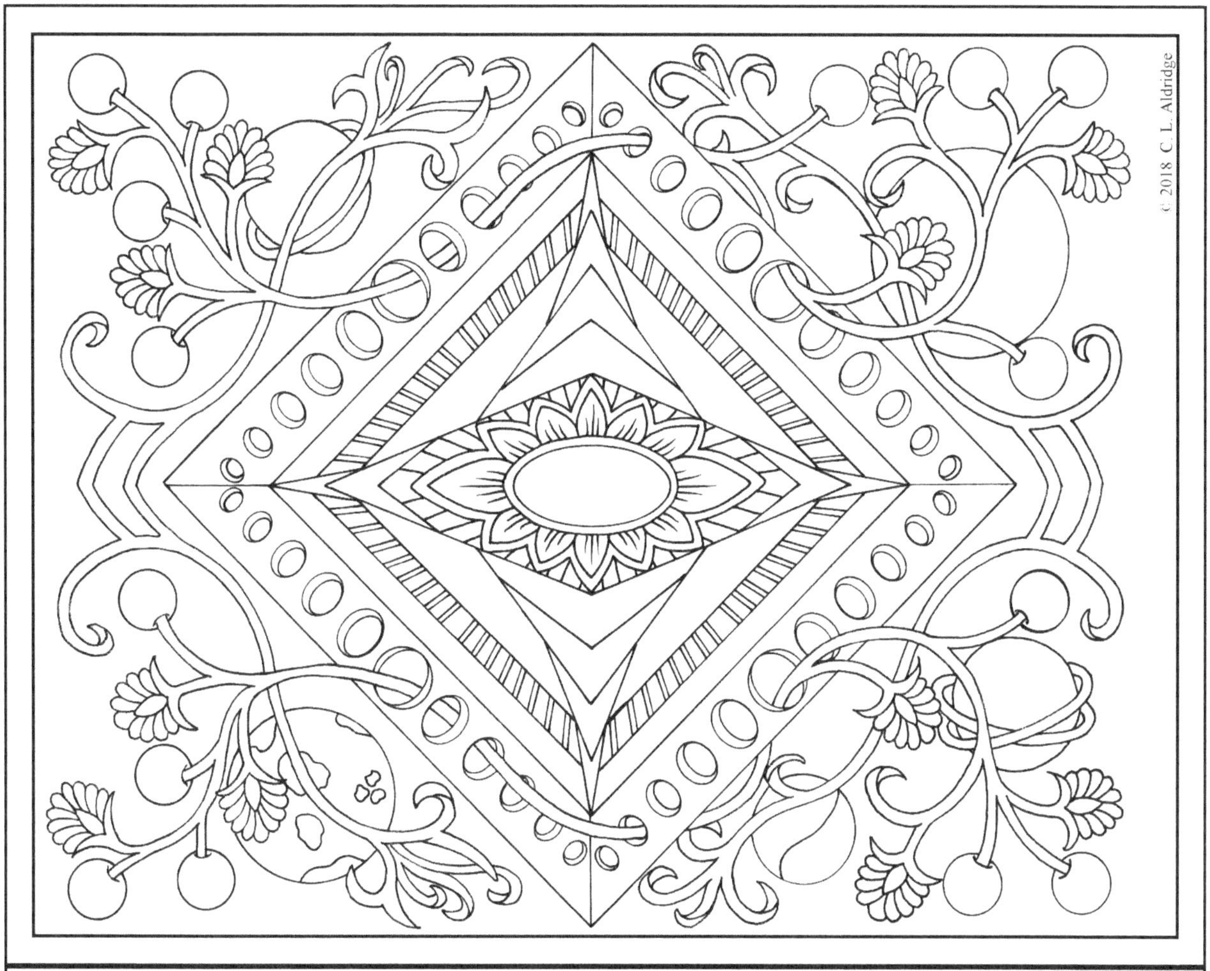

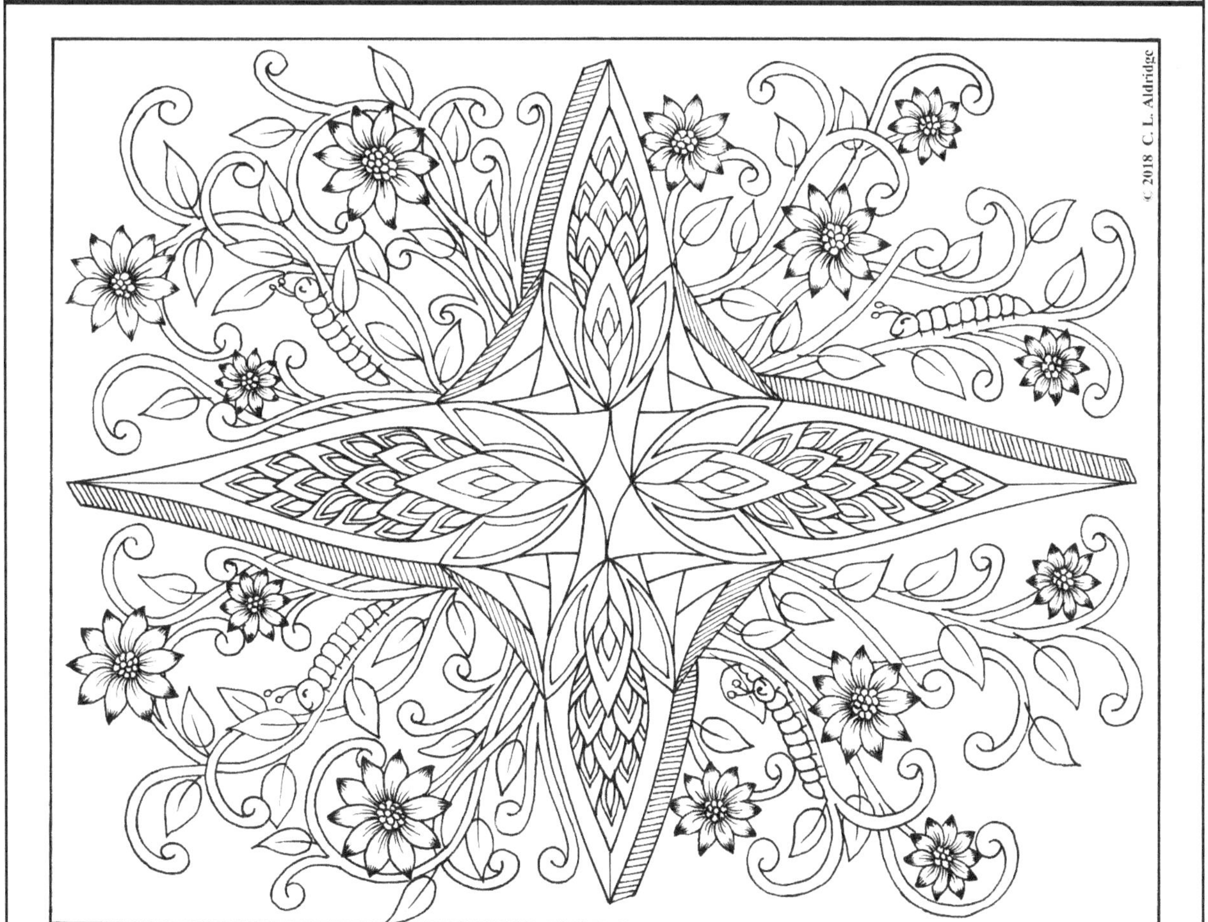

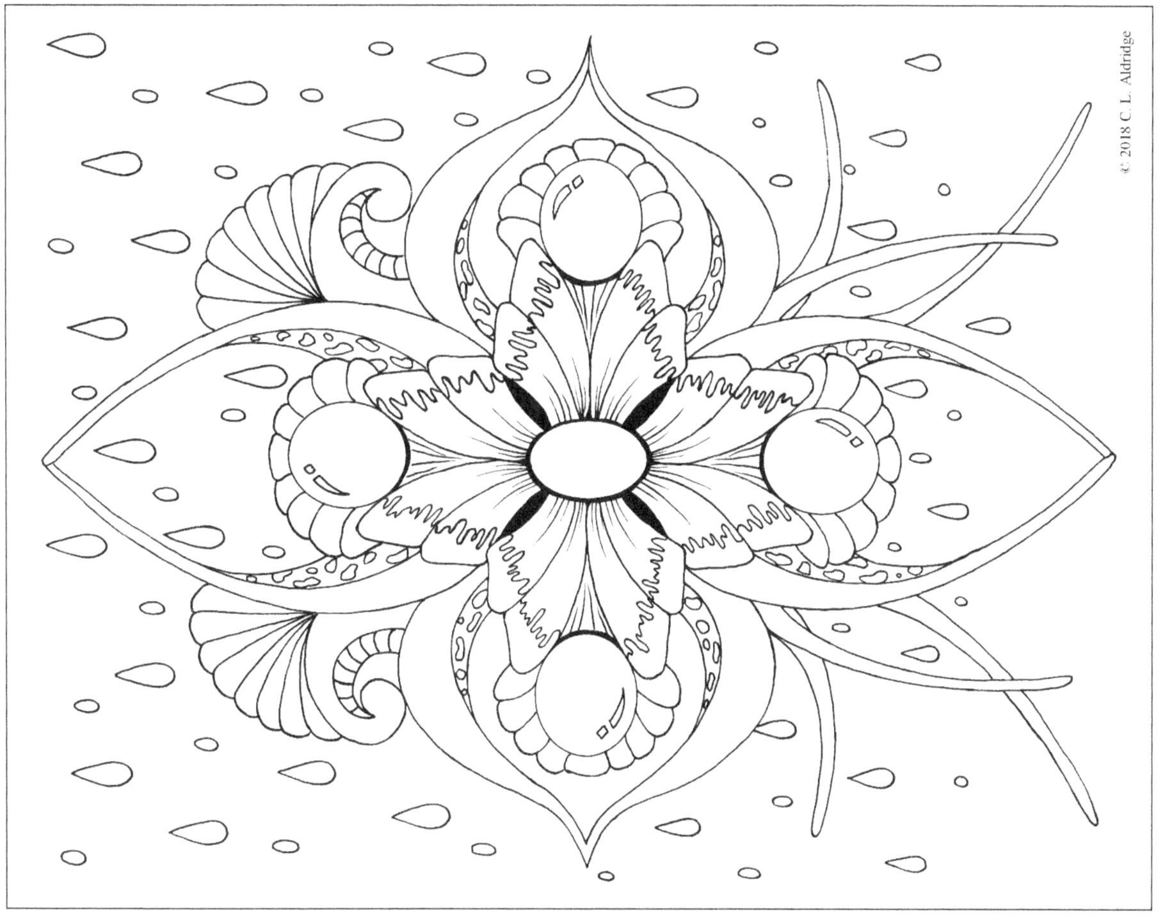

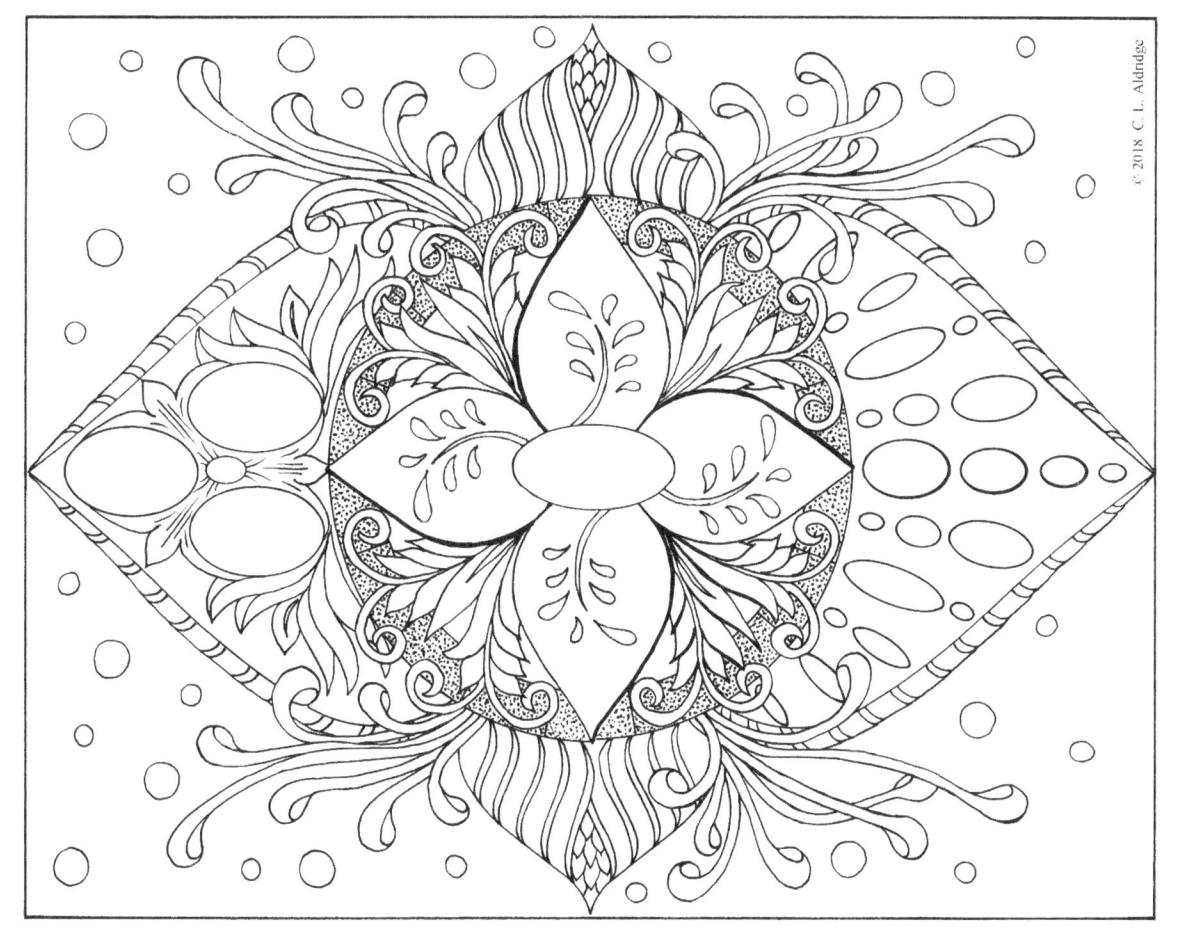

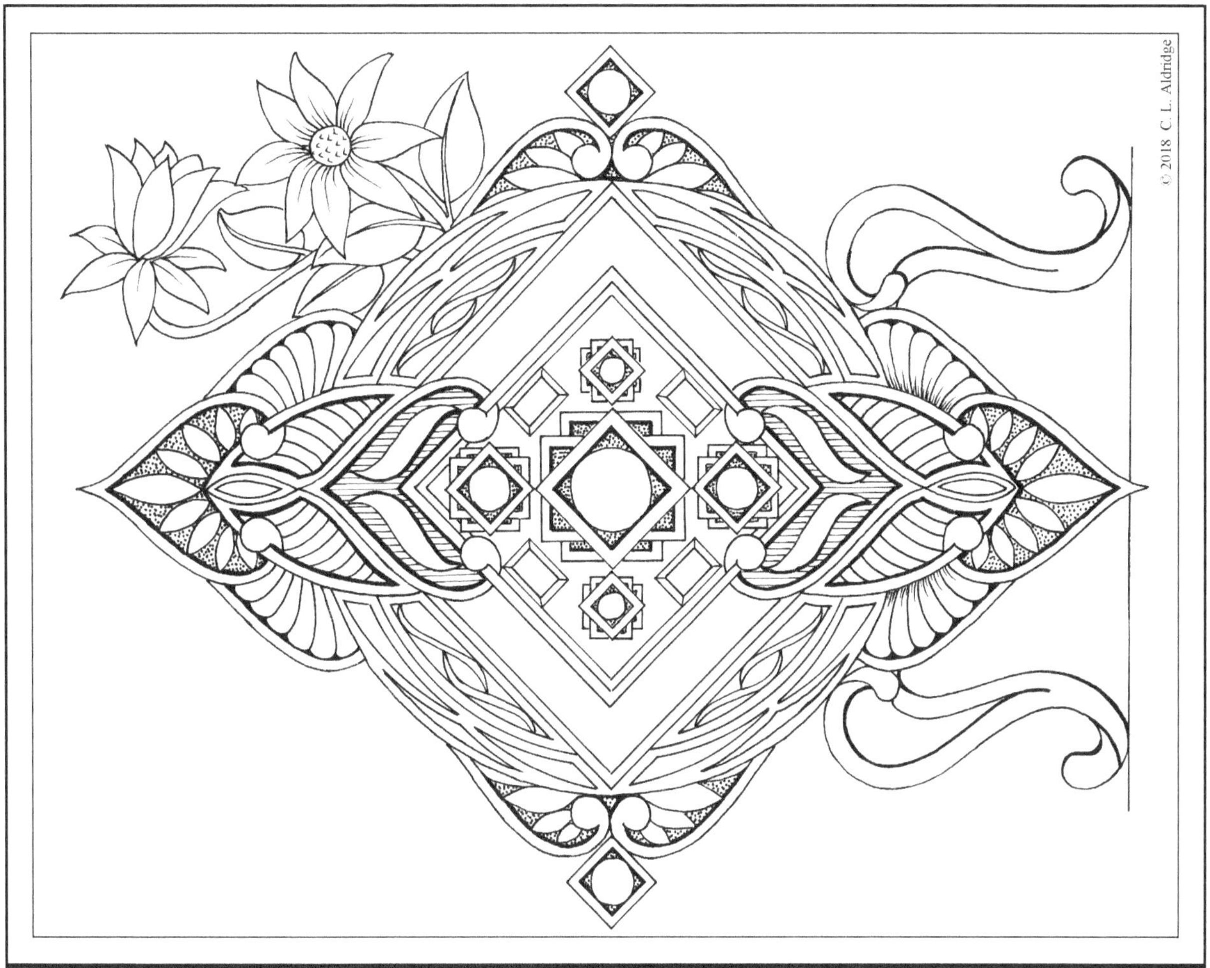

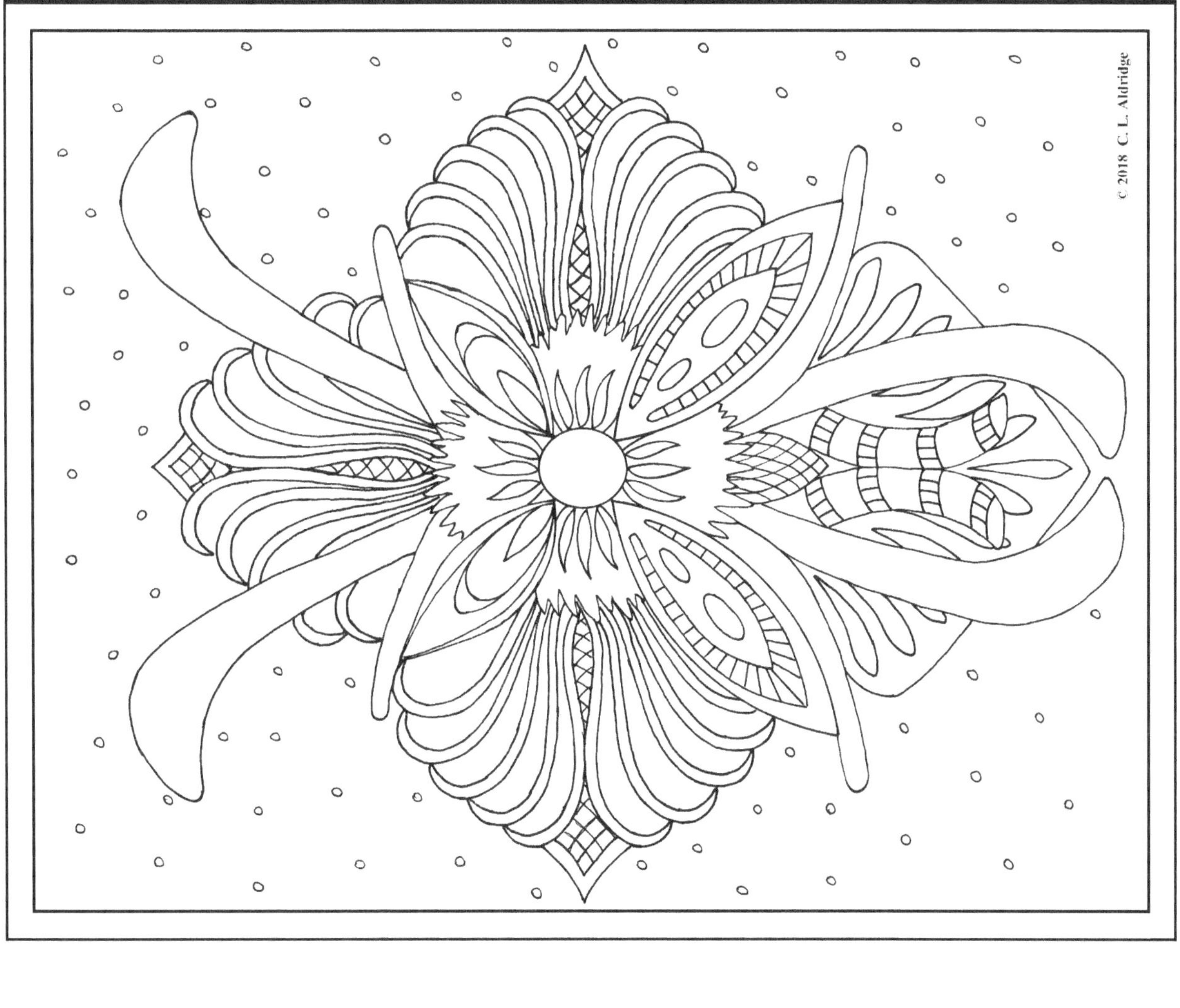

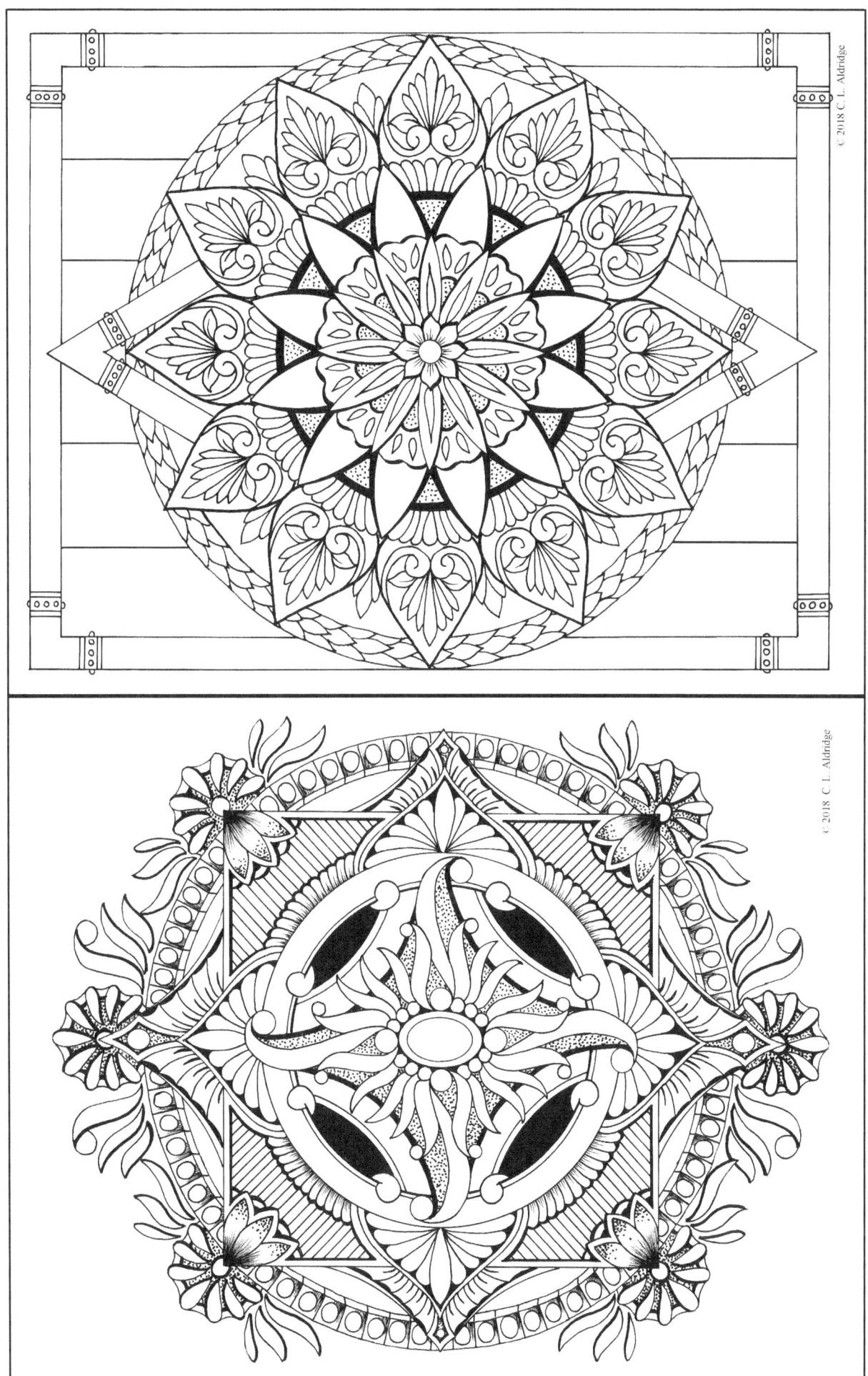

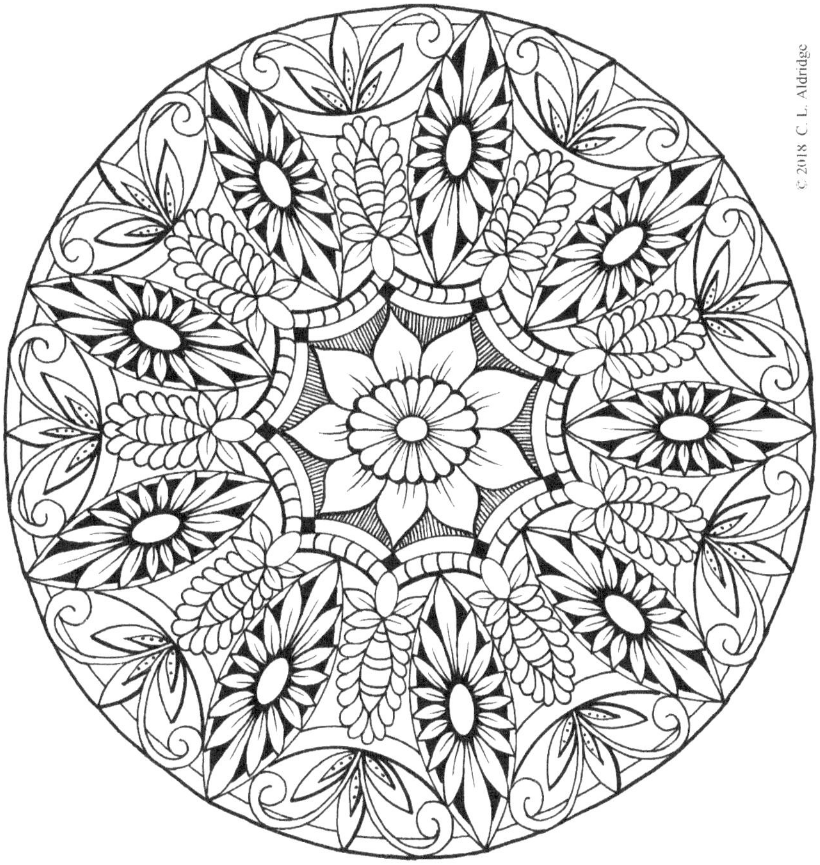

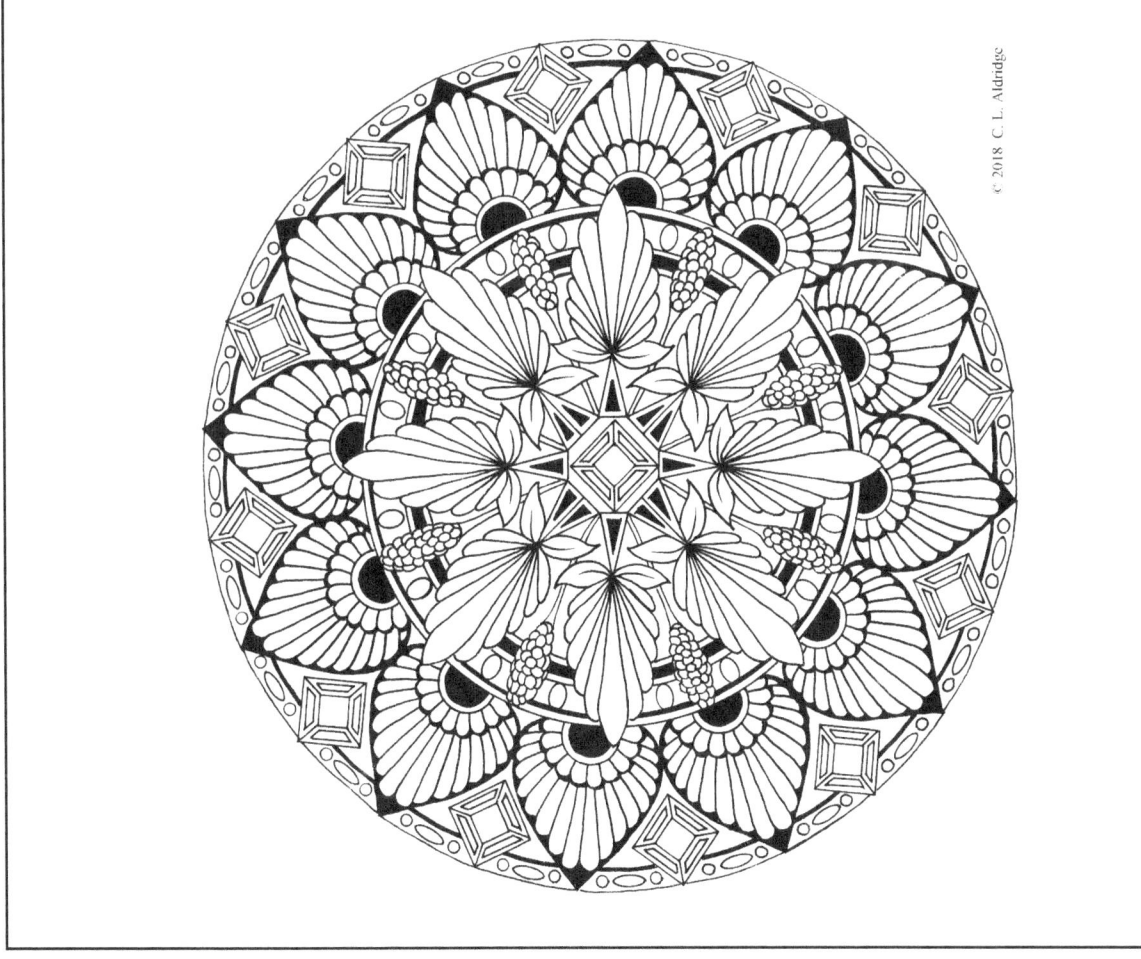

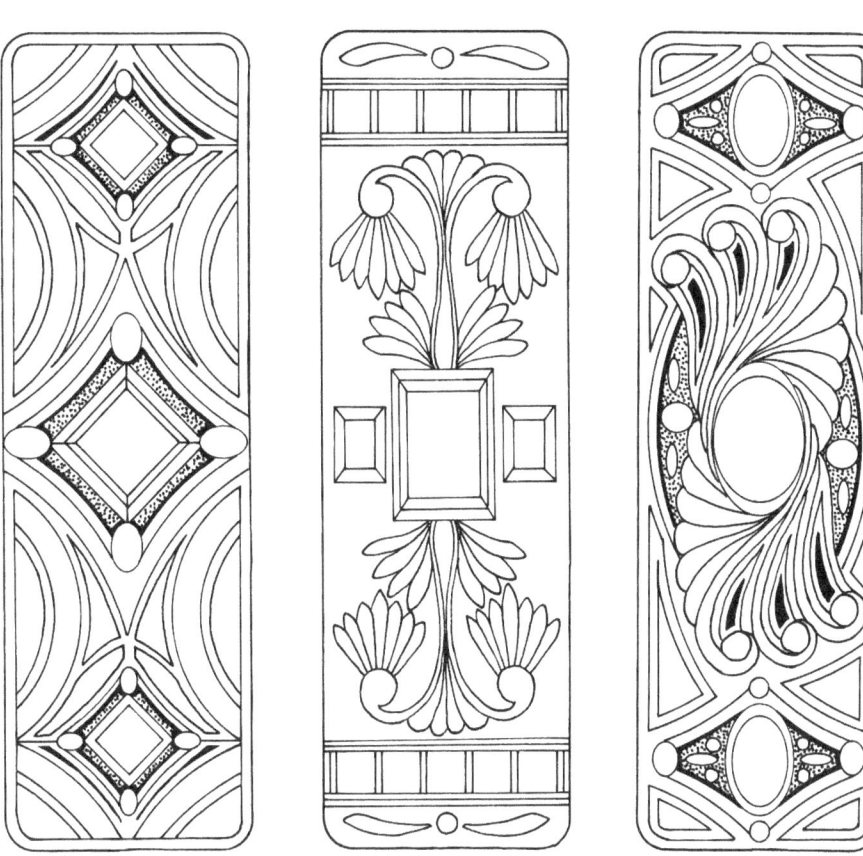

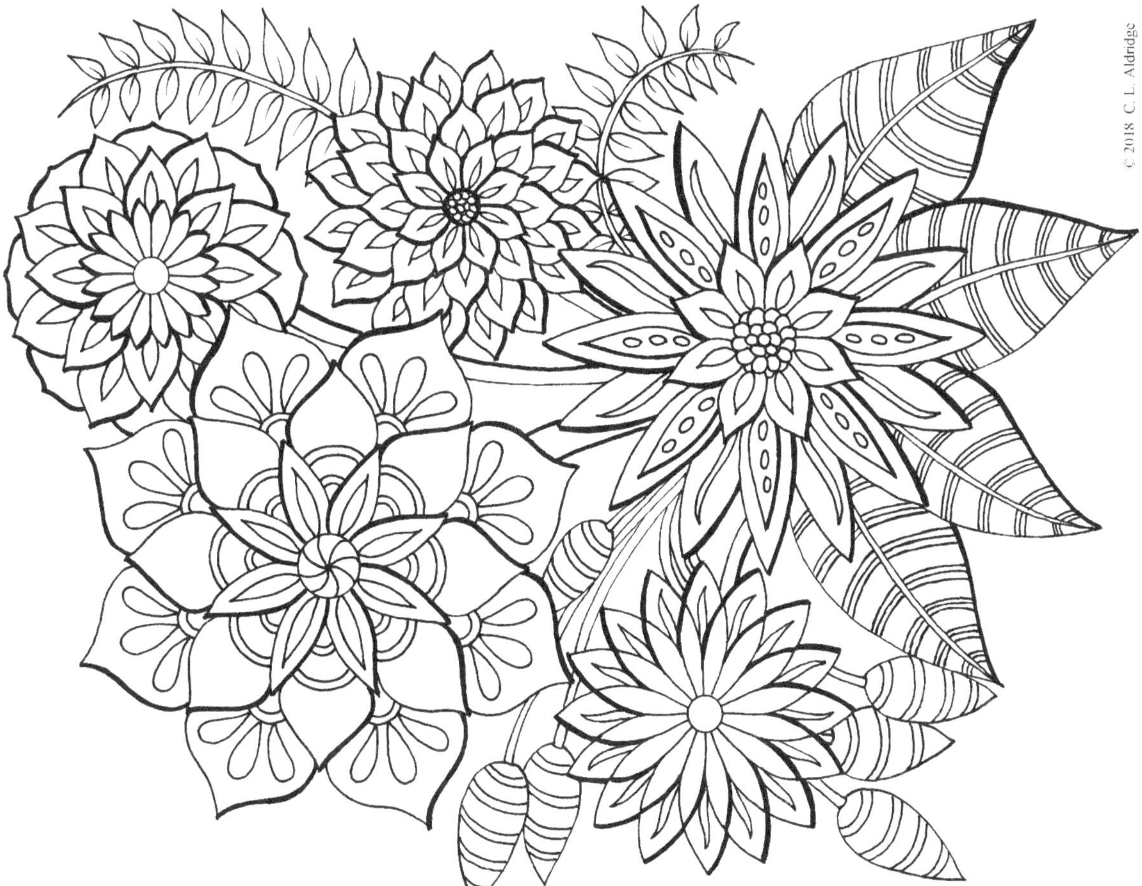

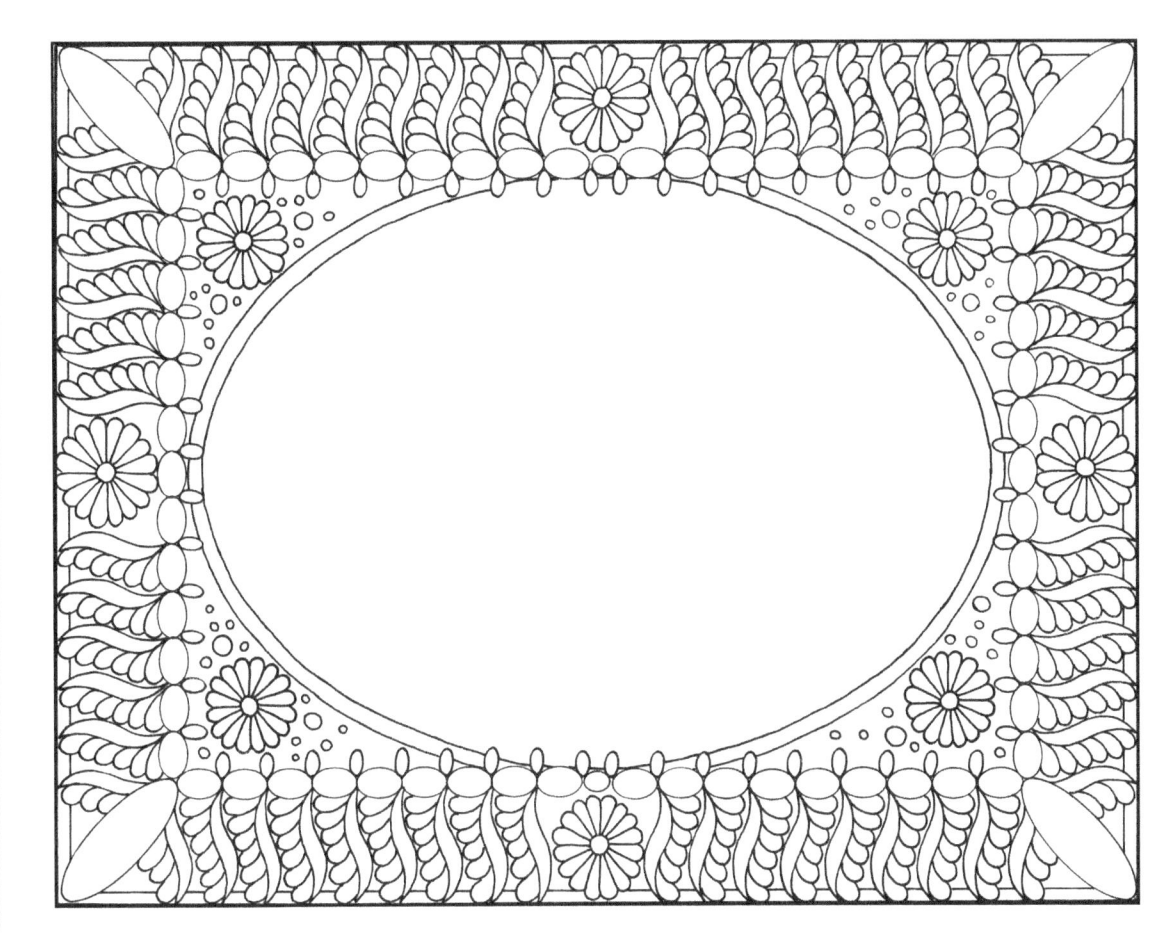
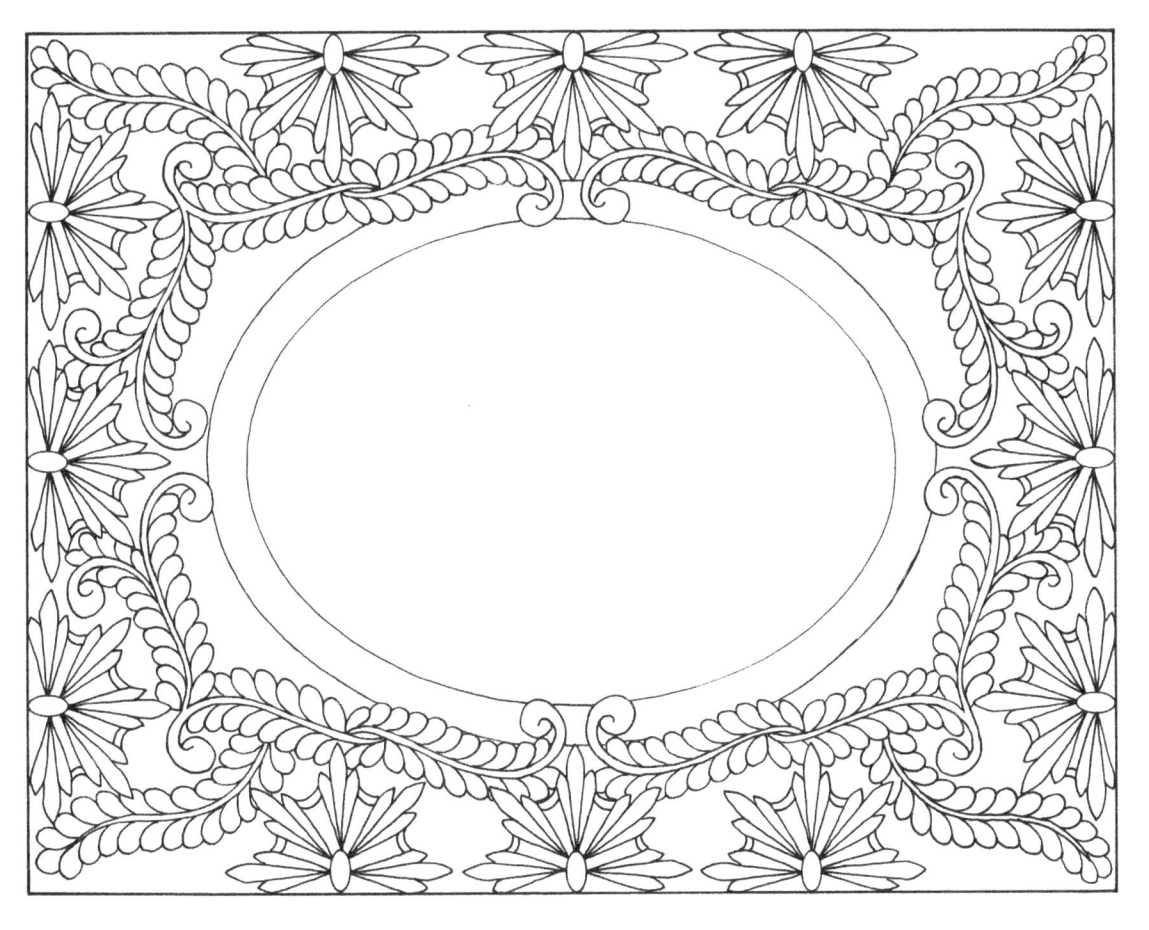

BONUS PAGES

In order of placement, a SAMPLE PAGE from the *also by* Adult Coloring Books of artist C. L. Aldridge:

"Flowers and Dreams"
"The Adult Coloring Book of Flower Inspirations"
"Flowers and Flyers" *
"Flowers and Whimsy" *
"Flowers of Fantasy"
"Flowers of Wonder" *
"Fantasy Flower Garden" *

*travel/crafters sized

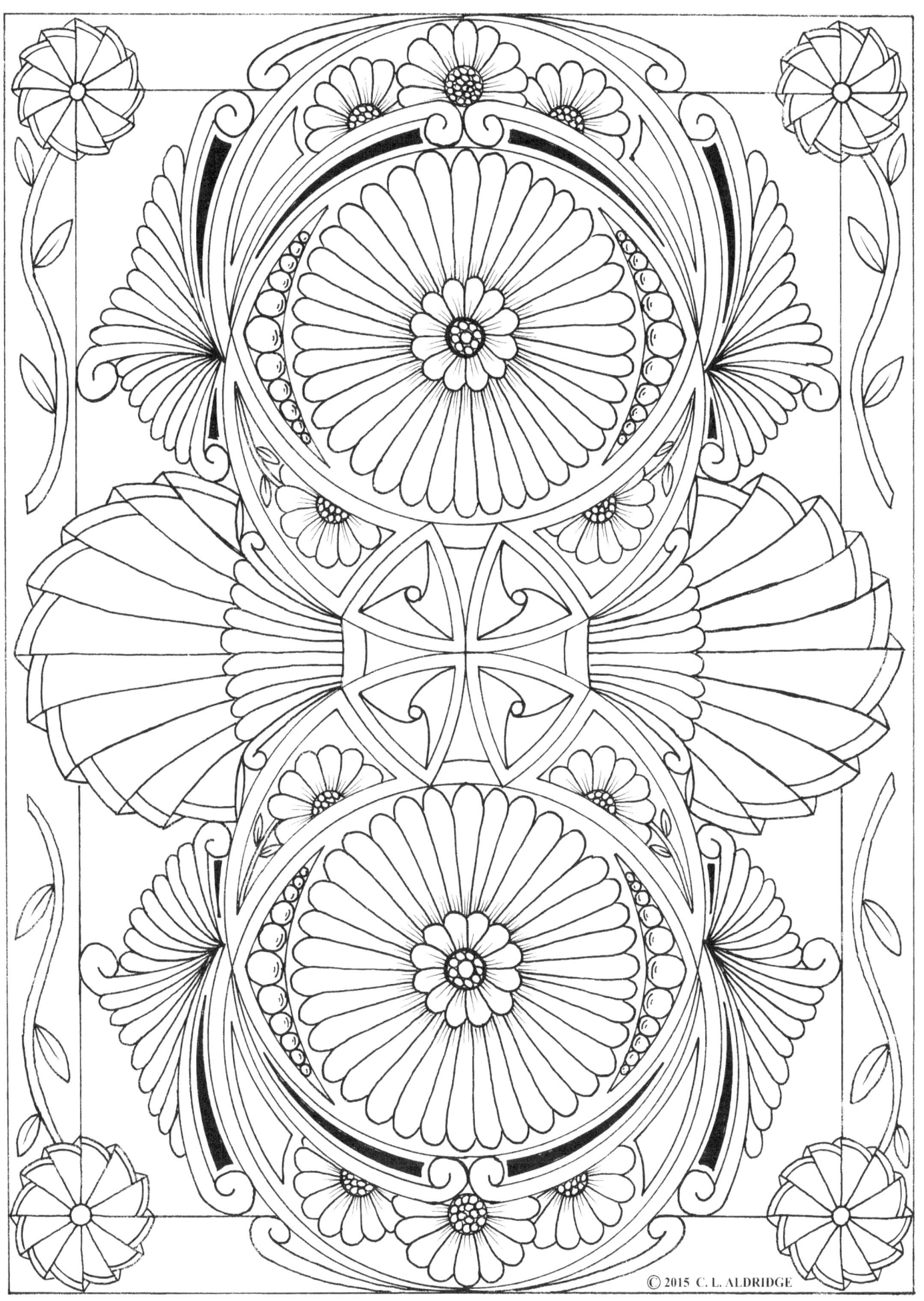

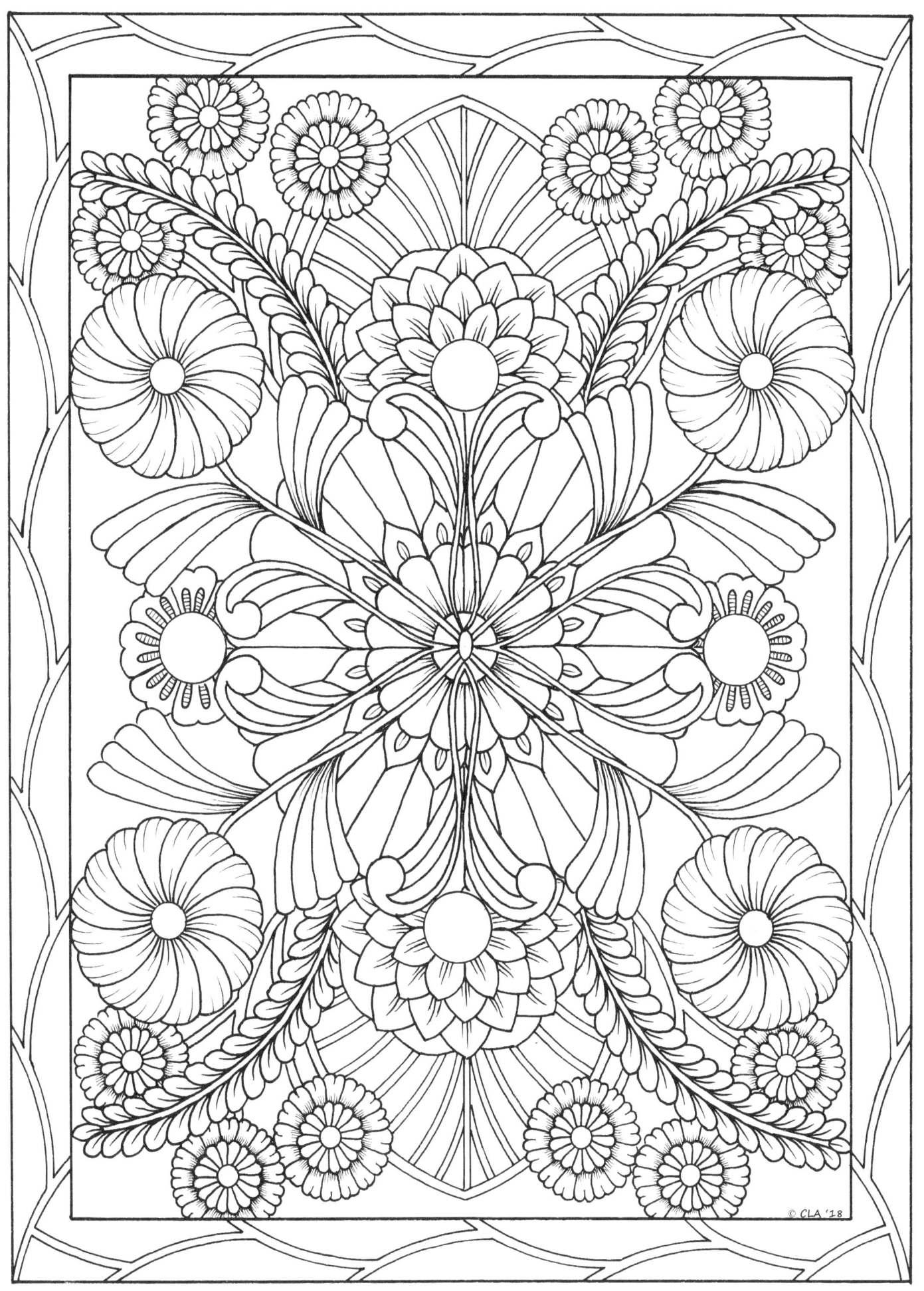

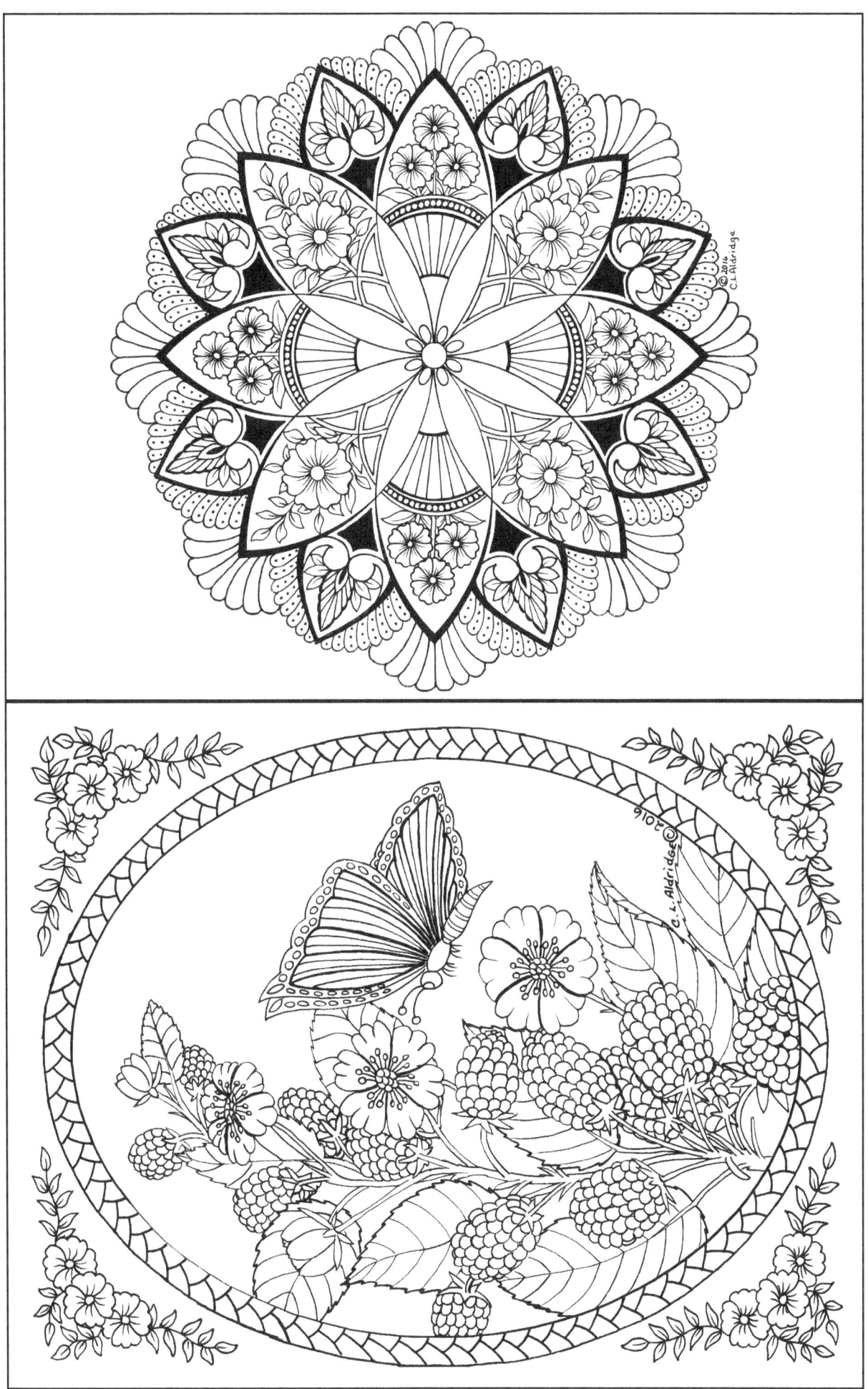

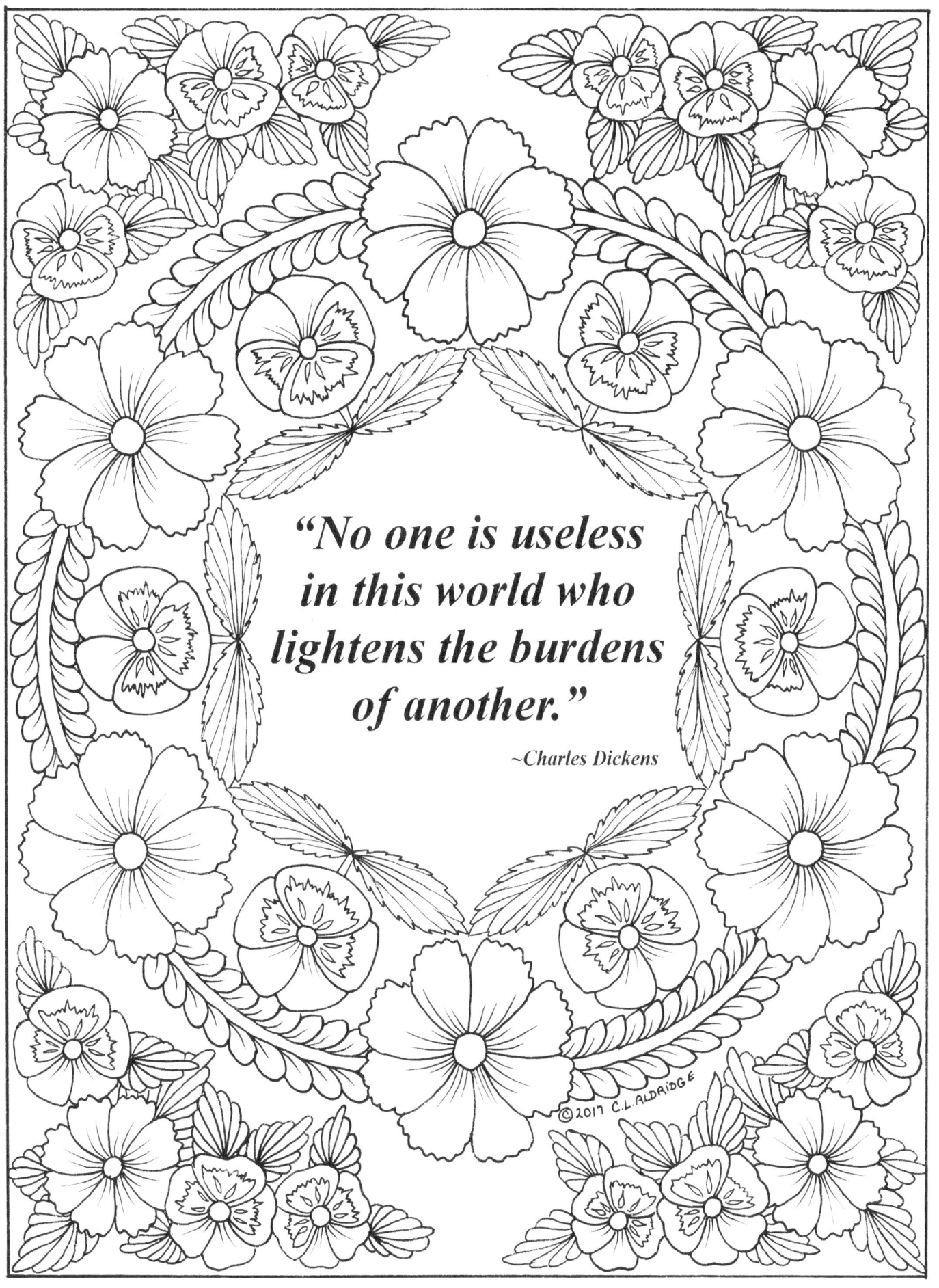

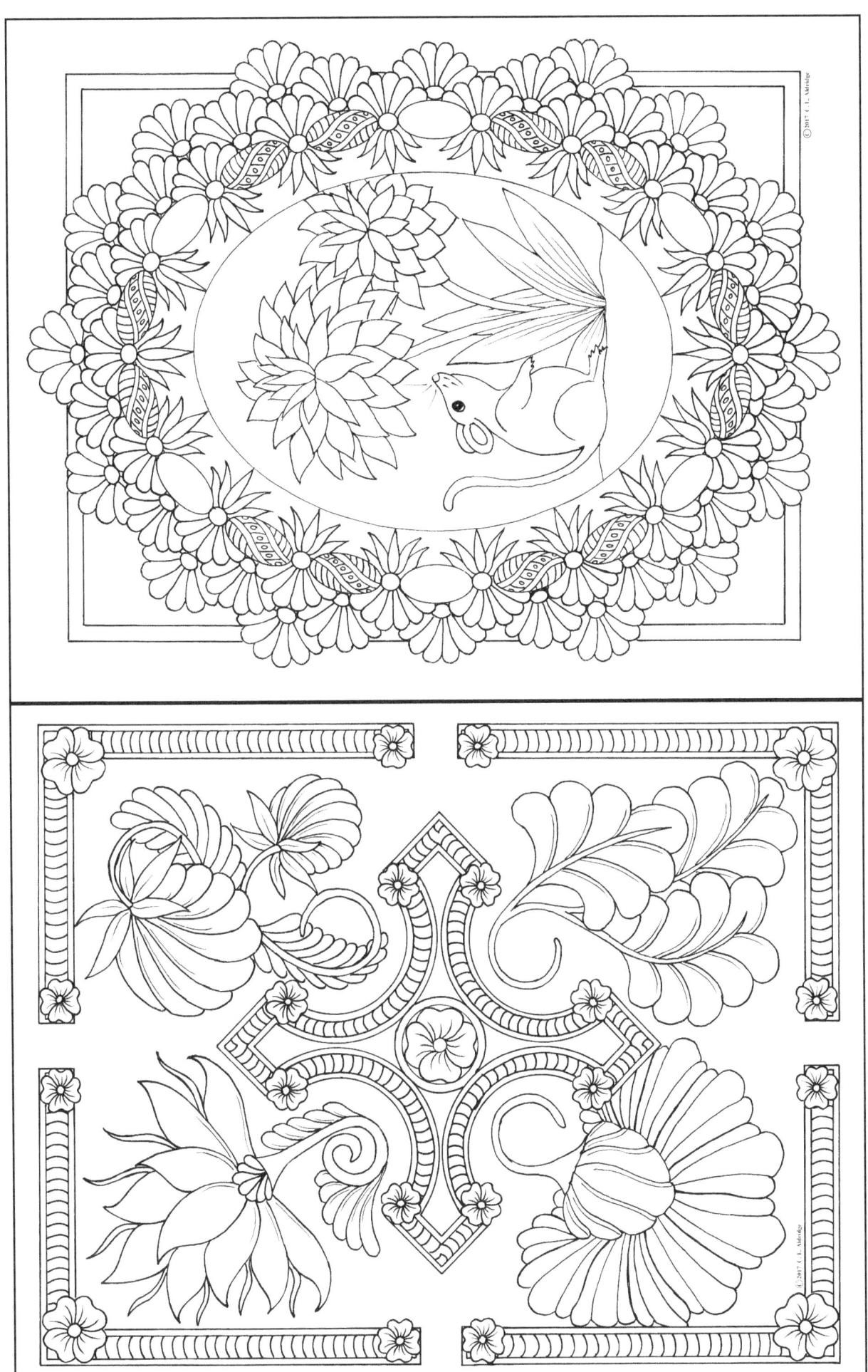

This page has intentionally been left blank for use as either a blotting page or color testing page.

Extraordinary Coloring Books for Extraordinary People

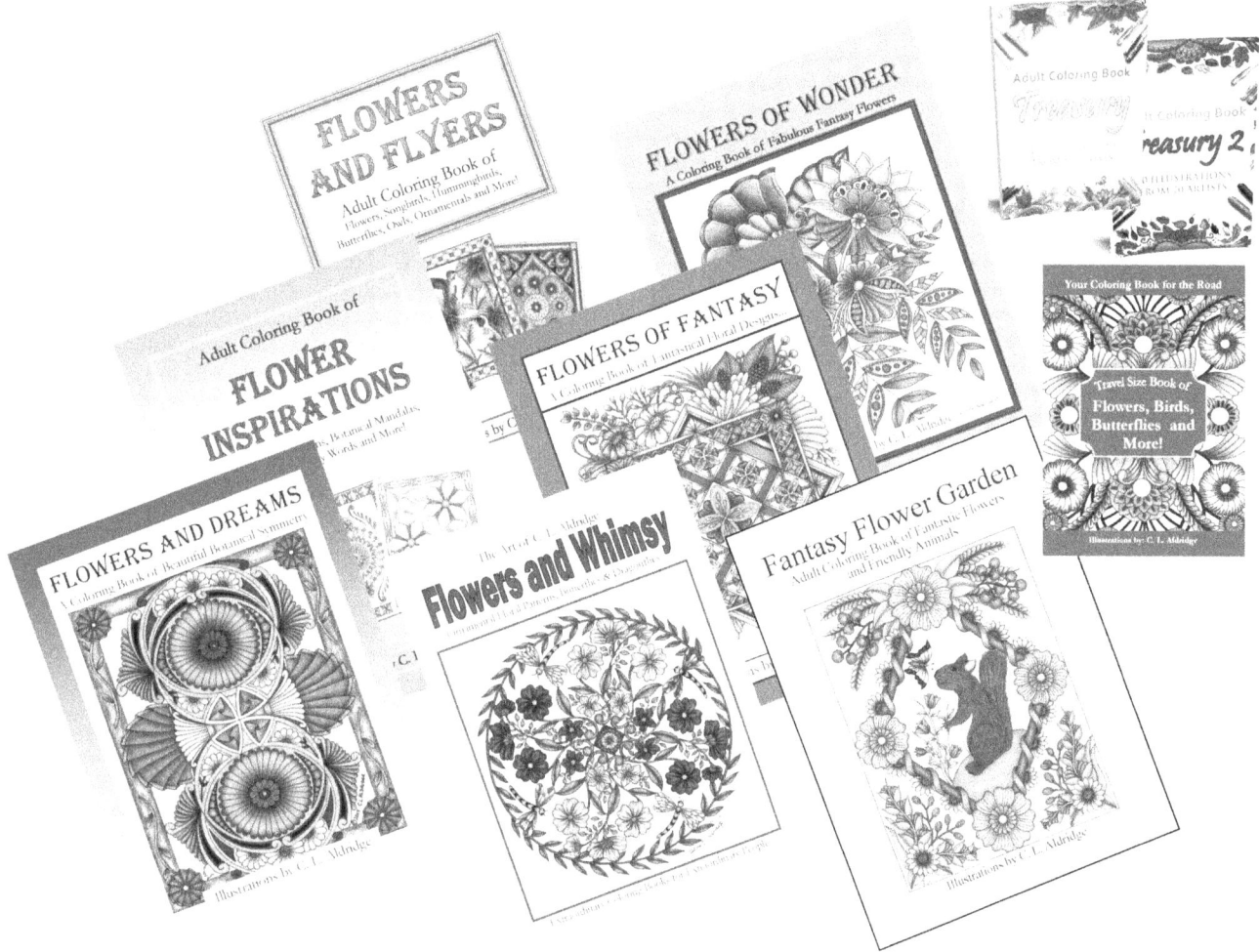

Available in Print at Amazon.com Worldwide
Full Books and Individual pages PDF's Instant downloads at CLAldridgeArt on Etsy.com

FOLLOW ME ON SOCIAL MEDIA AT:

Facebook, Instagram, Google or Pinterest as: @CLAldridgeArt

Visit my YouTube channel: CLAldridgeArt

or

Visit my website at www.CLAldridgeArt.com

www.ingramcontent.com/pod-product-compliance
Lightning Source LLC
Chambersburg PA
CBHW062330220526
45469CB00008B/2651